flow®

GET EVERYONE MOVING IN THE RIGHT DIRECTION ...AND LOVING IT

TED KALLMAN & ANDREW KALLMAN

NEW YORK

LONDON • NASHVILLE • MELBOURNE • VANCOUVER

Flow

Get Everyone Moving in the Right Direction...And Loving It

Published in New York, New York, by Morgan James Publishing. Morgan James is a trademark of Morgan James, LLC. www.MorganJamesPublishing.com

The Morgan James Speakers Group can bring authors to your live event. For more information or to book an event visit The Morgan James Speakers Group at www.TheMorganJamesSpeakersGroup.com.

ISBN 9781683506454 paperback
ISBN 9781683506461 eBook
Library of Congress Control Number: 2017909896

Cover and Interior Design by:
Chris Treccani
www.3dogcreative.net

In an effort to support local communities, raise awareness and funds, Morgan James Publishing donates a percentage of all book sales for the life of each book to Habitat for Humanity Peninsula and Greater Williamsburg.

Get involved today! Visit
www.MorganJamesBuilds.com

Disclaimer

All rights reserved solely by the authors. The authors guarantee that all contents are original and do not infringe upon the legal rights of any other person or work.

However, as with any book that spans multiple years, projects and/or assignments, we recognize that there is the risk that biases may emerge due to memories being colored by the passage of time. The case studies shared in this book are not quantitative research, but rather qualitative tribal stories meant to illustrate the elements of Flow as we have experienced them.

The original stakeholders, in almost all cases, have moved on to other roles and/or organizations. As such, their memories of the same events may or may not align with our takeaways and lessons learned. In fact, some of the organizations no longer exist.

Not all memories are pleasant. We have tried, to the best of our abilities, to frame our learnings in the most favorable light possible for all involved. The limitations of the written word, however, can lead to potential misunderstandings. It is also possible, in some cases, where decisions were made by leadership to take paths that we would not have recommended should not in any way be construed to reflect negatively on those leaders. We accept the prerogative of organizational leadership to make decisions based upon information to which we had no access. At the same time, we have tried to be transparent in our recollections and depictions of the events.

Many fear-driven organizations do not allow or accept this type of feedback. Our hope is that together we can find a better way forward and that all of the organizations mentioned in our case studies or the main body of this book will achieve and maintain a state of high-performing Flow.

To the best of our knowledge and understanding, the authors are not under any enforceable non-disclosure agreements (NDAs) regarding the information shared in this book. The viewpoints and opinions expressed in this book have been Distilled from working with these organizations during the past four decades and are ours alone. These views do not necessarily reflect or represent the views of the publisher, stakeholders, or other participants.

No part of this book may be reproduced, shared, and/or transmitted in any form without the written permission of the authors.

Foreword

As the futurologist for the Volvo Car Group, my area of focus is anticipating and forecasting where the future of Technology and IT is going. I spend my time exploring what that future will look like, primarily through the lens of technology. However, I also have had the privilege of observing trends in management and management theory. Through this lens, I have witnessed organizations experiencing pain as they work to migrate the benefits and value of new management methods, like Agile and Scrum which have proven to be successful at the team level. They are not, however, realizing the same level of success at the enterprise level.

Volvo Cars has experienced some of this pain.

As a reaction, we began using numerous organizational frameworks in various teams as an attempt to resolve these challenges. We have found these frameworks are a great start but they do not completely resolve the difficulties of scaling team level success to the enterprise.

Years ago, I had the privilege of working closely with Andrew and Ted on a project in Helsinki, Finland where these problems were removed or resolved using their unique and powerful frameworks, methods and practices. The amazing results realized by the utilization of what they now call Flow can be seen in the case study for the DNA Finland project in Appendix A. I have personally used elements of Flow that I learned in Helsinki for the past 17 years both individually and with the teams and organizations that I have led.

As we look at the future of continuous disruption and acceleration in the technology sector, the business side of any organization needs adaptive, flexible tools and practices that will move with the speed of cultural change without losing the disciplines necessary for quality and product integrity.

Flow is what's needed.

This book is the starting point for your journey in Flow. If you begin implementing what you will learn in this book, the result will be individual, team and organizational high-performance.

This is not theory.

It is results Driven performance that has been proven in organizations across the globe in many business and national cultures. This simple, elegant and powerful framework has delivered over $100 million net/net value to clients in Scandinavia, Europe, the US and Asia during the past two decades. I have personally experienced how it operates and have seen its massive, positive impact and potential.

The most remarkable thing to me is how down-to-earth and easy to communicate this framework is. In fact, it is so simple that it can be described quickly on a napkin over a cup of coffee and immediately understood and implemented.

Steve Jobs once said in Wired magazine that, "Simplicity is the ultimate sophistication." But, getting to simple is not easy. Many times, it takes years of experience, effort, focus and reflection (forged in the fires of reality) to achieve simplicity. This is precisely what Andrew and Ted have accomplished with Flow and the UVF (Unified Vision Framework). I would not be surprised at all to find, 10 years from now, Flow being the de facto standard for organizational governance and leadership.

I am proud to have been a small part of this story and expect amazing things to appear in the future as Flow becomes a household word in the business community.

As a futurologist, I believe Flow is the future of management.

ARIC DROMI
Chief Futurologist
Volvo Car Group
Gothenburg, Sweden

Introduction

Where does Flow begin? It begins with you. How do you optimize yourself to assure that you are operating "in the zone" or "in Flow?" How do you then migrate your "Flow" to others in the organization? Can you accelerate the creation of business value by using frameworks, tools, and methodologies?

It seems that everyone today in business or organizational management is constantly looking for the Rosetta Stone, secret sauce, silver bullet, or miracle cure that can be easily applied at night, with no greasy residue or foul odors, and in the morning – presto – problems and conflicts disappear and high-performance magically occurs.

Sorry.

You will not find a secret password buried in encoded messages on these pages. What you will find is a set of practices that have proven effective at Delivering high-performing results for individuals, teams, divisions, and organizations across the globe. We draw examples from our personal practice and a wide range of authors to show how high-performing results have been achieved. And, more importantly, how you in turn can follow this path and, combined with leadership and skill, obtain exponential results as well.

For the past 30+ years Ted Kallman and Andrew Kallman have Distilled, cultivated, and refined a set of practices known as the Unified Vision Framework (UVF) into what we now call Flow. "Flow" is the successful utilization of the UVF at all levels of an organization to help it create and maintain a state of high-performance.

The UVF began as a couple of tools and methods that Ted originally referred to as "the Model" which he utilized as an entrepreneur, manager, and business owner.

Flow, in its current iteration, is a methodology agnostic, business leadership framework for the executive, portfolio and program levels of an organization; and, when properly applied, effectively Cascades throughout the entire organization creating a state of high-performance and Flow at every level.

We share our Definition for Flow at the beginning of chapter 1.

The benefits of the UVF have been realized in Europe, Asia, and the USA in diverse organizations that were using Agile, Scrum, Lean, Six Sigma, Theories of Constraints, Balanced Scorecard, Waterfall, as well as other homegrown frameworks and methodologies. In most instances, the application of the UVF caused the organization with which we were working to improve.

Many times, it occurred exponentially.

We have tracked the value-add of using the UVF for many of these organizations during the past two decades. The total increased revenues, cost savings, and risk mitigation created by the UVF is in excess of USD $100 million in value-add.

The underlying team-level or project management Delivery approach that an organization uses is less important than you might assume. Success comes down to having a clear Vision, with the Right People, using clear Definitions, and Distilled agreements combined with a cogent Delivery plan that iteratively drives success Delivering outstanding value to the organization. This is why the UVF is methodology agnostic, and its implementation successfully cuts across industries, methodologies and culture (both national and company). When properly engaged, it has dramatically improved the bottom line for businesses and non-profits worldwide regardless of management style.

For the past few years, we have also applied the **UVF** in the new and emerging field of Agile (Scrum, Kanban, Lean, etc.). Agile and Scrum methods are realizing between 200 to 500% increases in productivity for teams all over the world. And yes, the **UVF** has helped make Agile methods more successful.

If you are not familiar with Agile thinking, we recommend you read the Agile books in the list compiled by Spotify for those interested in becoming great Agile Coaches:

http://www.cessan.se/2015/03/things-i-wish-i-knew-before-i-became-an-agile-coach-2/

The speed at which business and technology are changing is disrupting and transforming every part of our culture and economy. If you approach the new world economy with old world management tools (based on unsound principles or those that cannot adapt to the new reality), you will be left behind. For example:

> "To get a gut feeling of Moore's law, let's look at the physical evolution of the microchip. In 1958, a scientist at Texas Instruments developed the first-ever integrated circuit. It had two transistors (the more, the better) with a "gate process length" (the smaller, the better) of about ½ inch. This scientist would go on to win the Nobel Prize. In 1971, Intel came out with its first commercial product, a 4-bit CPU called the Intel 4004 integrated circuit. The 4004 had 2,300 transistors with a gate length of 10,000 nanometers, and computer power of about 740 KHz. By this time, each transistor cost about $1, on average. Now fast forward another 40 years. In 2012, Nvidia released a new graphical processor unit (GPU) with 7.1 billion transistors, a gate length of 28 nanometers, and processing power of 7GHz. The cost of a transistor: ~ $0.0000001. In just 40 years, the technology experienced a 100 billion-fold improvement, right on schedule for Moore's Law." [2]

PETER DIAMANDIS

This summary graphically explains the disruptive speed of change we are experiencing as a culture today. We cannot afford to maintain allegiance to management structures, frameworks, or methodologies that are not structured to allow rapid change. Technology has reached a profound state of high-performance. Our personal, team, and enterprise performance needs to mirror this.

There are many books and studies that demonstrate or explain how one enters into and maintains a state of personal flow. For example, one of the most often quoted and referenced researchers in the field of personal flow in the past 40 years is Mihaly Csikszentmihalyi. He states:

"To summarize briefly the essential conditions for flow to occur, they are: clear goals that can be adapted to meet changing conditions; immediate feedback to one's actions; and a matching of the challenges of the job with the worker's skills." [3]

We will quote Mihaly, Daniel Pink and his book "Drive," and many other authors to help the reader understand the hows and the whys of personal flow, how it fits or does not fit, and how it is not allowed to fit due to current management practices and beliefs. One survey, by Towers-Perrin, an 86,000-employee company operating in 16 countries, showed:

"According to the study, a mere 14% of employees around the world are highly engaged in their work, while 24% are disengaged." [4]

GARY HAMEL

Disengaged people or organizations will never enter a state of flow or high-performance. You will see passion and Vision referred to often in our examples. As Professor Hamel describes the power of passion:

"Passion can make people do stupid things, but it's the secret sauce that turns intent into accomplishment. People with passion climb over obstacles and refuse to give up. Passion is contagious and turns one-person crusades into mass movements. As the English novelist E. M. Forster put it, 'One person with passion is better than forty people that are merely interested.'" [5]

GARY HAMEL

The Gallup survey we will cite in Chapter 2 regarding management engagement paints an even more dismal picture with 51% of managers being disengaged. If individuals and managers are completely unplugged and don't care, there is no way the organization will prosper, let alone enter into a high-performing state of Flow.

Speaking of managers, high-performing teams in the knowledge economy are not managed, at least not in the classic use of the term. You will see this as we describe Scrum and Agile teams and their positive impact and effect. Agile teams are self-organized, self-directed, and self-managed. While this sounds like a recipe for anarchy, the reality is increased organizational discipline, control and transparency, as well as increased productivity between 200 and 1000 percent. Not all Agile teams become high-performing. However, the structure and practices combined with personal flow Deliver incredible job satisfaction, alignment with organizational Goals and Objectives, and remarkable results.

We will also show you how divisions and functional areas benefit from the structure and practices used in Flow. In our practice, we have found an almost universal disconnect at this level. It is almost always assumed that the Purpose, Mission, Vision, and strategic objectives of an organization's leadership are automatically reflected at its lower levels. The reality is that segmented and segregated silos operate based upon localized projects and operational tasks, not upper-level Purposes. The work necessary for true alignment is rarely done. We will show the importance and impact of doing this important job, and the dilution that occurs when this work is not done.

Even having the upper level Purpose, Mission, and Vision done well does not guarantee that an organization will become high-performing. There is a leadership component that cannot be ignored. For example, an article about Kirk Cousins, quarterback for the Washington Redskins, shares the following leadership transformation:

"In preseason games, Gruden says now in explaining the decision, the offense just seemed to work better with Cousins. He was its natural leader. The change in Cousins traces back to a meeting with veteran quarterback Matt Hasselbeck at NFLPA meetings last March. Cousins asked him for leadership advice. "I think that team needs a general," Hasselbeck told him. "They don't need a president. Try to be a

general, be authoritative and have a command." For his first three years, Cousins had stayed in the shadows of the Redskins locker room. The Redskins were not his team to lead. Now he speaks more loudly, and he has unified a locker room that had been divided." [6]

When the Redskins changed to Cousins as their field leader, they experienced an incredible organizational turnaround. Cousins himself had one of the best years of his career and in the history of the Redskins organization and was ranked as one of the top five quarterbacks in the entire NFL. Leadership will always be core to organizational high performance.

Finally, we will hone in on some of the other conditions necessary for Flow to occur in the executive suite and the anti-patterns that stop it cold. One of the latest buzzwords these days is "innovation." Every executive is talking about it and wants their organization to become more innovative. However, they are looking for innovation in everything except how they actually manage. Thus, they are experiencing insanity according to Albert Einstein, *"Insanity: doing the same thing over and over again and expecting different results."* [7]

They want innovation to occur without changing their management practices or structure. This disconnect is reflected in business literature:

"A stroll through the pages of the leading business management confirms the steerage-class status of management innovation. Over the last 70 years, the terms 'technology innovation' and 'technical innovation' have appeared in the title or abstract of more than 52,000 articles. More than 3,000 articles have focused on 'product innovation.' The comparatively new topic of 'strategic innovation' (which includes terms like 'business innovation' and 'business model innovation') has been covered in more than 600 articles. Yet, taken together, articles on 'management innovation,' 'managerial innovation,' 'organizational innovation,' and 'administrative innovation' number less than 300, and nearly all of these focus on the diffusion, rather than the invention, of new management practices-a bias that's understandable only if you believe that it's better to follow than to lead." [8]

GARY HAMEL

We believe that changing how you manage and lead has a direct correlation to the Delivery of innovative and exponential results.

We have been asked numerous times during the past 15 years to write a book that shared how the **UVF** consistently achieves remarkable results and how to implement it. We began that process with "**The Nehemiah Effect,**" our number one bestselling book on Amazon (that is, number one in six different months, since it was published in February of 2014, in four sub-categories: 1. Decision-making, 2. Business, 3. Consulting and 4. Project Management). In "Nehemiah Effect" we shared the ancient foundation for being Agile. We ended the preface of that book by stating:

*"We are now living in the convergence of **technological** and **knowledge growth** never experienced by mankind at any time in our history. This is not change management or incremental adjustments to existing plans. This is disruptive, transformational change that requires new mindsets and new tools combined with seasoned wisdom."* [9]

Flow, the follow-up to **The Nehemiah Effect,** while primarily for the executive, portfolio, and program management levels of organizational leadership, will be useful as a map and mindset at any level you engage it. We have structured the book in the following sections that reflect the change in their roles that most executives and managers will be facing as they journey toward achieving an optimal state of Flow:

Section 1: What is Flow?

We start with Definitions by Defining Flow and share a story that describes the deep and profound impact of this framework.

Section 2: The Elements (i.e. must haves) for Creating, Entering and Maintaining Flow

Then, we jump into the "how to" steps required for our framework to result in high performance.

Section 3: Antipatterns Preventing Flow

In this section, we deconstruct specific impediments and obstacles that will prevent this framework from achieving the potential and hoped-for results. If your organization is in a current state of high stress or chaos, you may wish to start here. Map out the anti-patterns you are dealing with and obtain agreement that change is needed prior to initiating the positive elements of Flow.

Section 4: Conclusion

We conclude with the importance of training, coaching, and mentoring in successful organizational transformations.

Appendix A – Mini-case Studies

As recently as last week, the question has come up "isn't Agile an IT-centric framework or tool?" Because of that common misunderstanding we are including additional case studies that are non-IT examples. Flow has succeeded in many IT situations, but Flow also goes beyond IT and works in all parts of any organization.

Appendix B – Using Flow to Govern Agile

The first five sections of Appendix B expand on what we shared in "The Nehemiah Effect." These lay out the road map and change management challenges that an organization will face if they try to "scale" Agile as a holacracy from the bottom-up. Flow enables an organization to transform from both the bottom-up and top-down simultaneously.

We agree with George Orwell's observation in his 1946 essay "Why I Write:"

"Writing a book is a horrible, exhausting struggle, like a long bout of some painful illness." [10]

In addition to the struggle experienced in finishing this book, we are grateful for the positive feedback we have received from our friends in the Flow community.

It is not always easy to capture the nuances of a successful system. Hopefully we have adequately covered the material so that you, the reader, can understand what is needed to enter and remain in a state of high performance and Flow.

Welcome to **Flow**.

Preface

"A dream doesn't become reality through magic; it takes sweat, determination and hard work." [11]

(Ted) am not a person that dreams often.

However, when I do, they are usually interesting and sometimes informative. One of these dreams recently happened. Since it relates to organizational leadership, I felt it would be thought provoking to share it here.

The dream began in a suburban neighborhood where I was standing in a garage and a neighbor from across the street came over to say hello. We were having a discussion about the high costs and fees for consulting services that his company had recently experienced. I responded to his comment with a few questions and a challenge.

Here's the dialogue from the dream:

Me: Your team has eight people on it, correct?

Neighbor: Yes.

Me: So your baseline costs or operating burn rate is around $100,000 per team member per year, so roughly $800,000 per year for the team. That breaks down to around $67,000 per month for the team, right?

Neighbor: Yes.

Me: So, what is the value that your team Delivers to the company? What was the net value-add for your last project?

Neighbor: Around $4.5 million.

Me: And, how long did that project take?

Neighbor: One year.

Me: So, let's analyze this.

What if instead of 4.5 million it was only $1 million per year of value Delivered by your team? That would be just over $83,000 in total value-add per month Delivered by your team – or a net $16,000 of value-added each month after subtracting the cost for your team to operate. This would be a net/net of $192,000 of value-add for the year. Correct?

Neighbor: Yes.

Me: Well, what if the value-add were $2 million with the same team? Now you have almost $167,000 of value-add per month with the same cost basis, so the net/net value-add would be around $100,000 per month. Or, $1.2 million in net/net value-add for the team for the year.

However, at $4.5 million your actual total Delivered value is approximately $375,000 per month for a total monthly net value-add of around $308,000. That's almost $3.7 million of net/net value-add for the year that was created by your team.

Does that seem accurate to you?

Neighbor: Sure.

Me: So, I have a question for you. Let's assume that your team is currently Delivering at the USD $1 million per year value-add level. If I, as a consultant, could through my skill, talent, and experience help your team move from $1 million to $4.5 million in value-add, would you be interested in engaging my services?

Neighbor: Absolutely, but it would depend upon your fees.

Me: Precisely. My normal daily rate is $3,000 per day. If it took me 12 months to Deliver the increase in net/net value-add from $192,000 to $3.7 million, then that would be an investment of $780,000.

Neighbor: Ok…?

Me: Would it be wise for your company to invest $780,000 to increase the net/net by $3.5 million?

Neighbor: Of course.

Me: So, what if I could Deliver the same result in six months, but the cost remained the same at $780,000, would that still be the same value-add to your organization?

Neighbor: Yes, but…

Me: Well, what if it only took 30 days? Would it still make sense for your company to engage me?

Neighbor: Yes, but I don't like where this is going…

Me: Now you're starting to get it. But let's go one step further.

Neighbor: Ok…?

Me: What if I could Deliver $3.5 million in value, but it only took one day to do it? Would it still make sense for your company to invest in my services?

Neighbor: Yes, but my CFO probably would not sign-off on paying you $780,000 for one day of consulting.

Me: Yes. And that's because most people do not understand the difference between cost versus investing in value-add. If an investment of $780,000 makes sense for a year's worth of consulting effort, then it also makes sense for one day of consulting effort, because it has nothing to do with duration. It has everything to do with the actual value Delivered.

And then I (Ted) woke up. That was the dream. But, it's not just a dream. It's also true. And, I'm currently still looking for that 1-day $780,000 gig.

But, the discussion should not be about cost and fees. It should be about value-add and how quickly it can be achieved. Most of the examples you will read about here in Flow were accomplished in relatively short timeframes, but with huge net/net value-added to the organizations. These organizations invested costs and fees for bringing in our expertise (not quite $780,000 per day). However, they all realized a significant net/net value-add.

We have Distilled our experience and methods into our books and we are confident that if you apply this knowledge correctly, you will experience similar results in similar time frames.

We have found that the principles, frameworks, and methods outlined in Flow can be learned and applied by anyone with consistently positive results. Our strong desire is to help initiate the outbreak of high-performing Cultures via Flow.

To that end, we have found that a few days of intensive training (assuming that the participants have the skill, talent, and experience requisite for understanding and successfully implementing Flow) will accelerate the speed at which results are obtained.

Once you understand Flow, you can Deliver Flow.

The higher your skill level, the faster you will see results. But anyone and everyone can benefit from applying the elements of Flow.

We look forward to hearing back from you on how your adoption of Flow has Delivered similar outstanding results.

Ted and Andrew

Shorthand, Abbreviations, Acronyms and Capitalization used in Flow

t is always a challenge to not use jargon or language that is specific to a methodology, framework or way of working. We capitalize and use the following shorthand, abbreviations and acronyms throughout Flow (for the most part) as follows:

- ☐ Flow
- ☐ Vision – "to be" in the future
- ☐ Mission – the business we are in (and, are not in)
- ☐ Purpose – the higher meaning for which we are working
- ☐ Values & Attitudes
- ☐ Goals & Objectives
- ☐ UVF – Unified Vision Framework
- ☐ VSPT – Vision, Strategy, People, Tasks
- ☐ 4D Model
    - o Define
    - o Distill – agreement on the definitions
    - o Deliver
    - o Drive

- ☐ 4R Model
  - ○ Right Ideas
  - ○ Right Values & Attitudes
  - ○ Right Actions,
  - ○ Right Results
- ☐ Agile
- ☐ Scrum
- ☐ Traditional
- ☐ Waterfall
- ☐ Cascade
  - ○ Cascading Vision
  - ○ Cascading VSPT
  - ○ Cascading "one thing"
- ☐ Epics
- ☐ Themes
- ☐ Features
- ☐ User Stories
- ☐ Product Backlog
- ☐ Sprint
  - ○ Increment
  - ○ Time Box
- ☐ Sprint Planning
  - ○ Increment Planning
- ☐ Sprint Backlog
- ☐ Retrospective
- ☐ Review

For additional definitions, shorthand, etc., please see our website at www. pmobrothers.com, the Scrum Guide by Jeff Sutherland and Ken Schwaber; as well as the Scrum Alliance and Scrum.org websites.

Also, please see our first book, Nehemiah Effect, to gain additional understanding regarding our methods and frameworks.

Table of Contents

SECTION 1:

WHAT IS FLOW?

Chapter 1

Flow Defined

"Use a picture. It's worth a thousand words." [12]

TESS FLANDERS

Perhaps a mental picture would help frame our book in a more memorable fashion. If you have access to the internet, please take a minute and look at this video of an actor portraying Bruce Lee playing ping pong, with a twist. The actor uses nunchucks (a martial arts weapon that consists of two wooden handles that are connected by a very short chain link in the middle) instead of a paddle. See:

https://www.youtube.com/watch?v=SncapPrTusA

You may be one of the more than 20 million people have viewed this video on YouTube. If so, you probably had the same response that we did, "Wow! That was an amazing display of talent." Or maybe, "Man, how did he do that?!" Regardless of your understanding of martial arts and the skill level needed to pull off that demonstration, you walked away impressed by a professional who was "in the zone." The actor was in a state of individual Flow.

We will touch on aspects of individual, personal Flow in this book and will point you to a number of resources that can assist you in getting to, and staying in, optimal personal performance and it will not be a commercial created to appear like a high-performance professional at the top of his game. By following the principles of Flow, you will actually become a high-performing professional. Smoke and mirrors won't be necessary.

We will touch on team level flow by highlighting both the benefits realized and challenges faced by teams. Much of this discussion will relate to one of the strongest methodologies we have found for team high-performance, which is Scrum/Agile. By the way, a list of Definitions and acronyms included in this book will help you navigate any Agile-specific or project-management terminology used. You may want to put a sticky note on those pages to quickly reference terms or acronyms with which you may not be familiar.

We will spend the majority of our efforts dealing with optimizing Flow for the whole organization. This, of course, assumes that the underlying teams and individuals are all either in, or growing toward, a state of Flow.

Our beginning Definition of Flow is:

"The state of optimal performance achieved by applying a clear, consistent, persistent and unified Vision at all levels of an organization."

Here are some descriptions from other authors regarding Flow:

"The highest, most satisfying experiences in people's lives were when they were in flow … in flow, people lived so deeply in the moment, and felt so utterly in control, that their sense of time, place, and even self melted away. They were autonomous, of course. But more than that, they were engaged."[13]

MIHALY CSIKSZENTMIHALYI

"When we choose a goal and invest ourselves in it to the limits of our concentration, whatever we do will be enjoyable."[14]

MIHALY CSIKSZENTMIHALYI

Csikszentmihalyi correlates a state of personal flow with the word enjoyable. Daniel Pink utilizes Csikszentmihalyi's research as the basis of his book "Drive" and he depicts flow this way:

"One source of frustration in the workplace is the frequent mismatch between what people must do and what people can do. When what they must do exceeds their capabilities, the result is anxiety. When what they must do falls short of their capabilities, the result is boredom. But when the match is just right, the results can be glorious. This is the essence of flow."[15]

DANIEL PINK

"There is a way to get a grip on it all, stay relaxed, and get meaningful things done with minimal effort, across the whole spectrum of your life and work. You can experience what the martial artists call a 'mind like water' and top athletes refer to as the 'zone,' within the complex world in which you're engaged. In fact, you have probably already been in this state from time to time."[16]

DAVID ALLEN

"Rowers have a word for this frictionless state: swing ... trying too hard sabotages boat speed. Trying becomes striving and striving undoes itself. Social climbers strive to be aristocrats, but their efforts prove them no such thing. Aristocrats do not strive; they have already arrived. Swing is a state of arrival."[17]

CRAIG LAMBERT

"Technically, Flow is defined as an optimal state of consciousness where we feel our best and perform our best."[18]

STEVEN KOTLER

Flow is both a state of enjoyment and a state of arrival that results in high performance for individuals, teams and entire organizations. The quotes above are really great and we feel they reflect a deep understanding of some of the key positive elements and blockers for an organization that wants to achieve a high performing state of Flow.

For those that are interested, we will be sharing other books that focus on process optimization or product flow. For example, Don Reinertsen's book on

"Product Development Flow" is a superb resource since it gives the mathematical proofs and engineering viewpoint that analytical individuals love.

We have not included a Definition from Reinertsen's book "Principles of Product Development Flow: Second Generation Lean Product Development" in the quotes above, because we weren't really able to find a crisp Definition for "Flow" anywhere in his book. His book is a great tactical and operational resource and we love the math which validates the Unified Vision Framework (UVF). We have utilized his ideas related to proxy variables, queues and small batch size.

Not having a succinct Definition, in our opinion, muddies the Vision for his book. But, we have been able to piece together, from three different pages, some of the descriptions of how he views flow:

"At its heart, this new paradigm emphasizes achieving flow. It bears many similarities to the methods of lean manufacturing and could be labeled lean product development (LPD)—To distinguish this more advanced approach from the ideas of lean manufacturing, we call it Flow-Based Product Development—A flow-based process delivers information on a regular cadence in small batches." [19]

If you compare the cobbled-together quote above about flow from Reinertsen to the quotes at the beginning of the chapter, it becomes clear that Flow is important for individuals, teams, projects, products, divisions and enterprises to attain high-performance.

Reinertsen's focus is solely on product.

However, in addition to product development and individual Flow states, there are also group Flow states that apply to teams, projects and enterprises:

"There is also a collective version of a flow state known as 'group flow.' That is what happens when a bunch of people enter the zone together." [20]

STEVEN KOTLER

If you are looking for a book or framework that will help you optimize (or sub-optimize as the case may be) individual processes or products, then "Flow" may not necessarily be the book for you since our focus in "Flow" is on the whole picture.

For those of you that may not be familiar with Traditional, Lean or Agile methodologies, Flow fits in the picture as a methodology-agnostic, Executive tool to organize work:

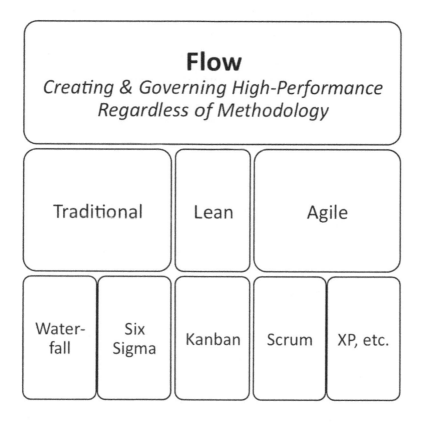

We will share how to achieve a state of high-performing Flow for individuals, teams and organizations; and, how the framework and principles of Flow can be applied to successfully improve any process or product.

We have included dozens of examples in Flow from the past four decades of how we have helped individuals, teams and organizations achieve higher levels of performance using the principles included in Flow.

The following story is a powerful picture demonstrating the impact of Flow.

A Stunning Example of Flow at SingTel

The following project case study is an example that demonstrates the immediate, powerful result of using Vision and the Flow framework at the team level. Take a moment to think about what you would do (using your knowledge, skill set and experience) to rescue the following project that was crashing and burning, and you have been given 90 days to successfully implement the changes and turn the project around. Here are the brutal facts:

- [ ] This was an infrastructure build-out that included Operational Support Systems and a marketing team that was supporting the targeted national brand launch.
- [ ] They were two years into a three-year project with a demoralized team of around eight people that were working 60 – 80 hours per week each.
- [ ] The project team leader from Deloitte had a Ph.D. in organizational behavior and had been on the project from the start. She was also trying to use the PMBOK (The Project Management Institute's Project Management Body of Knowledge), cover-to-cover, to try to Deliver the project, including:
  - o 40 "PMBOK" inspired reports issued weekly, monthly and/or quarterly, including status updates;
  - o And, an MS Project plan with over 2,000 lines of work activities and task level items.
- [ ] There were 440 Stakeholders and 38 Steering Committee members.
- [ ] The weekly, four-hour status update meetings, were shouting matches (sometimes in multiple languages) and rife with politics.
- [ ] The original schedule to complete this project was three years. We arrived two years into the original time frame. The estimate to complete this project, at the point in time that we arrived, had been extended to 5 years, total.
- [ ] The initial budget estimate had increased by 300% to pay for the additional resources and time needed to complete the project.

EXERCISE:

What would you do? Take five minutes and on a blank piece of paper or blank page at the back of this book, write down what tools, methods and/or frameworks (agile, traditional or otherwise) you would use to fix this problem. By the way, you only have 90 days to successfully complete your task of turning this project around. When your list is complete, come back and compare your list with the results of our turnaround efforts using Flow and the UVF.

Some of the responses we've heard when using this exercise in training situations have included:

- ☐ Fire everyone and start over.
- ☐ Look for quick wins and use the success to gain momentum for the team.
- ☐ Go back and get executive buy-in for the changes needed.
- ☐ Run away; you can't fix this.
- ☐ This sounds like the project I've been working on for the last six months.
- ☐ Time to update my résumé on www.monster.com.
- ☐ Etc.

This is a perfect example of where all of the key elements needed to create and maintain Flow in the work effort were broken, fractured or absent, and where the organization was struggling and obviously not getting their desired results.

On arrival, the following was the **assessment** of the "as is" situation for the project:

- ☐ The Vision was unclear and was creating Anarchy within the team, the SingTel organization and its multiple external stakeholders.
- ☐ We weren't certain if they had the Right People working on the project, but the Anxiety levels for both the team and its individual members was sky high and burnout or bailout was a real risk.

☐ The project Definitions appeared to be incomplete or incorrect, which led to Confusion for everyone, including the 440 stakeholders and 38 steering committee members and the Executive Sponsor.

☐ Worse yet, they had assumed agreement from all stakeholders instead of doing the work needed to Distill Agreement which led to Politics and disagreements.

☐ All of the issues listed above resulted in poorly executed Delivery and Chaos, both from a planning and reporting perspective.

☐ Anyone that has ever done any level of project management knows that you would never attempt to use the PMBOK (Project Management Body of Knowledge), cover-to-cover, to successfully Deliver a project. It is a great reference tool with a collection of good practices, but it is not a road map.

☐ And, as the pile of work and confusion grew exponentially, trust eroded, the team became more Divided and the sponsor was losing confidence in the successful Delivery of the project. All of this created situations that blocked Driving the project to a successful conclusion.

To sum it all up, what were we dealing with when we walked in the door was Anarchy, Anxiety, Confusion, Politics, Chaos and Division. It might have been wise at that point to take the advice that one of our students shared above and "run away!" but we didn't.

Our confidence, however, rested in the power of the Flow framework that had succeeded hundreds of times in turning bad situations around. It was an ugly scenario, but we had the conviction that this project could be saved.

So, instead of turning tail and running, we started with the project's Vision.

You have to work from the level you are at in the organization. Vision is always the key driver for what a project is trying to achieve for its product, service or result (i.e. increase revenues, decrease costs and/or get rid of or mitigate risk). If there is no project Vision, your job as a leader is to Define and Distill agreement on what the Vision really is (or should be) with the appropriate stakeholders. You must understand and articulate the "why" for your team.

Sometimes it is possible to get senior executive support and sometimes it's not. In this case, it was vital to the eventual success of the project. However, we didn't start out with the full support of the Senior VP who was in charge of this project at SingTel. However, he came around fairly quickly. Even if we had never obtained his full support, we still would have started with the project's Vision because that's how you focus a team on doing the Right Actions that will ultimately lead to high performance, regardless of executive buy-in.

The project's challenges made it clear that the project's Vision was fractured. And, upon closer inspection, this project was a poster-child for everything that could possibly go wrong.

Before heading to Singapore, Andrew made sure that he had complete buy-in from the executive leadership at Ericsson (his employer at that time) and Deloitte, including the authority to cancel the project, if necessary. Clearly, part of the stakeholder management in this case was to get buy-in from the senior vice president at SingTel, the sponsor for the project, to make the needed changes.

First, we reduced the number of stakeholders:

- ☐ The total number of project stakeholders were reduced from 440 down to "only" 38. (Originally, we had wanted to reduce it below 20, but the senior vice president wasn't willing to cut that deep.)
  - o Using the communications formula of n * (n-1) / 2 gives you the total number of communication channels for a team or organization.
  - o So, having 440 stakeholders at SingTel resulted in a total of 96,580 potential communication channels (i.e. 440 * (439) / 2 = 96,580)
  - o With that many possible channels, it is no surprise that the noise and politics had completely crippled the productivity of the project team.
- ☐ By reducing the stakeholders to 38, that reduced the potential channels down to 703
  - o Thus, a 91% reduction in the number of stakeholders resulted in a 99% reduction in the potential number of communication channels.

The senior vice president was reluctant, at first, to give Andrew the free hand needed to deal with the other stakeholders. But, there was really no choice.

Eliminating over 400 stakeholders from the project created quite a stir and the noise level and politics (both internally and externally with vendors) went up dramatically in the short-run. The "removed" stakeholders were ultimately kept in the loop via a newsletter.

By the way, if Andrew had conducted the Vision exercise that we usually do with the organizations with which we work, where everyone is given a blank post-it note to write the "Vision" for the organization and/or the project, word-for-word, we know from experience that there would be 500 versions of the project's "Vision" from the 440 participants. Moreover, we know for certain that the majority of the post-it notes would not have matched each other or, word-for-word, the overall Vision of SingTel. There was no unified Vision.

The word "division" in English literally means "two Visions." When you have two Visions, they don't necessarily line up with each other. Imagine having over 500 "Visions" that were out of alignment with each other. This gives a whole new meaning to the word "division."

Andrew worked with the team to align their project Vision into a short, easy-to-communicate Vision statement along the lines of "*enabling the successful launch of the Pod Brand.*"

With the team's Vision in place for the project, Andrew then started using the newsletter to inform the original 440 stakeholders of the project team's progress towards the project Vision. This mitigated the noise levels from the 400+ external stakeholders significantly. Andrew used Vision to kill off the anarchy.

The next part of the Flow formula was ensuring that the Right People were on the project team. Did they have the Right People on the project team? Apparently not; they were one or two people short. Initially Andrew was added to the team to assess whether or not the project could even be saved. He later added one or two additional team members, short-term, to support the project team during the 90-day turnaround period. Andrew also worked with Ted in the background and used him as a sounding board, mentor and coach to make sure he kept his focus on the big picture, so that he could rescue this project and Deliver it.

After meeting with the original project team, Andrew decided that everyone on the team was competent to Deliver the project. The team members themselves, however, were not as confident. In fact, most of them were very worried that they would be removed from the project. And, most likely, they were probably hoping that was the case after two years of exhausting work. They were also quite afraid that they were going to be fired from their respective companies due to the severe crisis that this project was in. The team's anxiety level was through the roof, and based on their performance to that point in time, they should have been worried.

Rebuilding the team included the following:

- ☐ The team was forced to reduce hours worked to only 45 hours per week instead of the 60 to 80 they had been doing.
- ☐ The original team leader was required to stay until to the end, as were all of the other team members.

"Is your time being spent primarily in activities that reinforce your Vision or directly contribute to the pursuit of your strategy? If not, then you're not focused enough. One sure way to force yourself to focus is to work less. JW Marriott, founder of the Marriott Corporation, had a useful philosophy that he applied to building his company from a single-unit restaurant to a major corporation: 'Work hard. Make every minute on the job count. Work fewer hours---some of us waste half our time.'" [21]

JIM COLLINS

Quantity of time worked does not equal quality. Some team members had somehow bought into the idea that more hours equals more output. But, the fact is the quality each individual contributes actually goes down if the team has been working at an unsustainable pace for too long. That was exactly the case with this team. The team was in total shock when Andrew told them that they would no longer be allowed to work 60 to 80 hours per week. He capped their time at 45 hours per week.

At first, they didn't believe him. But, Andrew started turning out the lights and locking the project room's door at 6 pm in the evening. He also monitored their online activity in case they were using any of the online tools in the evening to try to bypass the new rule. If he caught them in the system(s), he logged them out and gave them a call and had a chat. Within a week or two, the team adapted to the new pace. They actually started to get more done by working less.

This demonstrated the wisdom of the old Japanese proverb: "slow down to go fast." David Allen, who the magazine FastCompany calls the "personal productivity guru," puts it this way:

"In training and coaching thousands of professionals, I have found that a lack of time is not the major issue for them (though they themselves may think it is); the real problem is a lack of clarity and definition about what a project really is, and what the associated next-action steps required are. Clarifying things on the front end, when they first appear on the radar, rather than on the back end, after trouble has developed, allows people to reap the benefits of managing action." [22]

The team was mostly correct and complete in its structure. However, one of the main things the team was lacking was a battle-scarred veteran with enough experience and skill who could effectively manage the noise and politics by using a framework like the Unified Vision Framework.

One of the core tools of the **Unified Vision Framework (UVF)** is the **4D Model** (**Define** - D1, **Distill** - D2, **Deliver** - D3 and **Drive** - D4) and this was used to turn this project and team around:

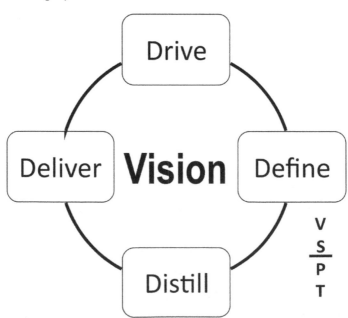

VSPT is an acronym for Vision, Strategy, People and Tasks and how we use it will be addressed shortly.

Having put the Vision in Place and identifying that we had the Right People on the team, the next steps were to use the 4D Model to turn the team around, get them focused and Deliver the project. This included training, coaching and mentoring the team. The UVF training, coaching and mentoring for the SingTel team lasted 90 days.

Initially, not everyone on the team was on-board with the change. The team leader even laughed when Andrew walked her through the UVF. She simply could not comprehend how Vision could be used to turn the situation around. Although she had a Ph.D. in organizational behavior and had all of the requisite "textbook" knowledge, she just didn't have the hands-on experience and/or battle scars that are crucial to understanding the power of Vision and simplification.

Achieving Flow at the team level requires leadership that has the right experience and team members that have "been-there-done-that" and who have demonstrated the ability to simplify processes. Fixing a team or project can be done quickly with the Right People using the right tools – like Flow.

We will take a quick detour here from our SingTel story to make a point on how quickly Flow can impact an organization. We had a maintenance director of a large non-profit that went through our one-day training session on the UVF and the very next day began implementing the 4D Model. He emailed us about a week later to let us know that using the Unified Vision Framework had completely and radically transformed his entire organization at lightning speed. He shared that he had used the first two Ds – Define and Distill – to clarify and manage the executive team's constant changes to his departmental scope and Deliverables. He also reported that the executives themselves loved and appreciated his new approach of requiring clear Definitions and clean agreements.

So, is simplification really valuable to the enterprise?

Yes!

A thunderous, resounding YES!

Another example, involves a client with whom we reduced the lead time for identifying project requirements for one of their project teams from 18 months to three months. Also, for another high performing team, we helped them reduce their project lead time from 18 months to one month – yes, by a factor of 18 to 1 – by simply applying Flow to a single process.

How much was that worth in value-add to the organization? Almost USD $4 million. Not only were there significant financial benefits, but also this customer was better positioned to bring new product/features to the market almost a year earlier than before. It is stunning that this company had been paying almost USD $4 million above what was needed because they had over-complicated their requirements gathering process and were thus releasing product(s) much later than planned.

In fact, keeping it simple is very hard to do, and it can be an excruciatingly painful exercise for many organizations. Culture eats process, particularly any new process, for breakfast, lunch and dinner. Legacy and traditions are the twin bulldozers pushing culture forward. It doesn't take any special skill set to make things more complex than they already are. Anyone can do that. Warren Buffet observed that:

"Business schools reward complexity. Simple is more effective"[23]

Spot on: simple is more effective.

However, simple is definitely not easy.

After observing the results Andrew achieved at SingTel during the first four weeks, the team leader realized that she should not have been laughing, but rather listening, learning and implementing the changes needed. Doing things "by the book," simply doesn't work when flames are all around you and engulfing your team. "Theory" alone could not put out this inferno. She, her team and their respective organizations had experienced a brutal reality and learned it the hard way. The same team delivered this project seven months early and $4 million under budget by entering into a state of Flow high-performance. The balance of the SingTel story is shared throughout the remainder of this book.

Chapter 2

Elements of Flow

The UVF (Unified Vision Framework), VSPT (Vision Strategy People and Tasks), 4D Model (Define, Distill, Deliver and Drive) and the 4R Model (Right Ideas, Right Values & Attitudes, Right Actions and Right Results) cut across all of the following elements that we include here in Flow.

This includes communication, having a common language and creating a shared Vision. Training, tools, technology, business content, relationships and crowd control also impact Flow and need to be considered in every area. Let's start with Vision.

Simplicity, Clarity and Focus on Vision

"Simplicity is the ultimate sophistication."[24]

STEVE JOBS

To achieve the eventual seasoned, mature simplicity of high performing organizational Flow you must start with Vision. Vision must be crafted in simple language that is easy to remember and communicate. And, Visions tend to diverge over time as an organization grows and prospers. It's the nature of the beast. Peter Drucker summed up this natural entropy well by stating:

"Only three things happen naturally in organizations:

Friction,

Confusion, and

Underperformance.

Everything else requires leadership."[25]

Leadership requires prioritizing and honing the Vision down to the "one" thing on which the entire organization should focus. In our experience, most company Vision statements are not clear or easy to remember. They are not memorable because they are too long and, as a result, not actionable. Also, most enterprises and organizations do not, to a large extent, Cascade their Vision from the top-down as shown on the right side of the following picture, indicated by the "one" in the circle:

Cascading Vision: the One Thing

The Vision should be the one thing that is most important to the organization. It is the white-hot why and cannot be multiple things.

The reality is that the further you are from the C-suite, the less clear the Vision usually is because of the lack of clarity mentioned above. It's not for a lack of desire. It's just that it is never thought of in this way (it's assumed that it has already occurred) and thus rarely done.

How do you achieve a sophisticated simplification?

We always begin with clarifying and simplifying the Vision statement first. It should be no longer than five to seven words. Any statement longer than that will result in high levels of dilution as the leadership attempts to communicate that Vision throughout the organization. The upcoming graphs demonstrate the severity of this dilution.

Most organizations assume that they are successfully Cascading their Vision from top to bottom. Research across the board shows that this is a fallacy and that the upper level Vision is rarely clear at the task level. And, even fewer organizations are able to link-back the Vision (via intentional actions) from the team level back up to the organizational leadership level.

The grim reality is that even if you lose only 10% of the clarity at each organizational level (as the Vision Cascades through it), by the time you get to the individual team member you have already lost almost half (47%) of the original Vision:

CASCADING VISION - FLOW DILUTION @ 90% OF CLARITY RETAINED PER LEVEL

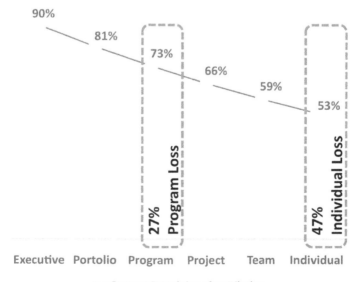

In these examples, the Organization is six levels deep (to reach the team member level) and the percentages are the percent remaining after dilution.

At the Program level in the example above, 27% of the original Vision is at risk of having been Diluted. This is probably one of the better arguments for flattening an organization, since the fewer levels you have, the less Dilution of the Vision can occur.

At an 80% level of clarity (a 20% loss in clarity per level; an 80/20 Pareto ratio), by the time you get to the individual level you will have lost up to three-fourths (74%) of the original Vision, so, around half (47%) of the original Vision is at risk of having been Diluted.

At a 50% level of clarity, you have gridlock; and, only a 2% chance that the original Vision makes it through to the Individual delivering tasks to fulfill that Vision:

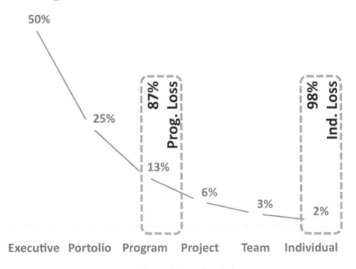

CASCADING VISION - FLOW DILUTION
@ 50% OF CLARITY RETAINED PER LEVEL

50%

25%

87% Prog. Loss

13%

6%

3%

98% Ind. Loss

2%

Executive   Portolio   Program   Project   Team   Individual

– –Percent Remaining after Dilution

These examples are stunning.

At the Program level, in this example, almost all of the original Vision (87%) is at risk of having been lost.

The second image above (the 50% dilution level) is what we find to be the best case in most organizations when we begin to work with them. The ability of an organization to effectively and accurately communicate its Vision to all levels is not a "nice-to-have," it is a matter of life or death.

For many years now we have advocated the use of what we call the "Cutting Room Floor" / Forced Prioritization exercise (i.e. prioritizing the work at the Board, Cxx, Executive and Director levels).

This involves taking the entire backlog of work (i.e. Programs / Projects) that needs to be done and going through a few rounds of editing (i.e. cutting). If you start with 25 items in your Executive backlog, then the first round of cutting should eliminate 80% of the items. That is only 20% make it through the first round of cutting. So, you go from 25 backlog items down to 5 items.

The second round of cutting follows the same idea that 80% of the surviving 5 items are eliminated and you are left with one item in your backlog. This is your "one thing." This is the item on which you focus the organization:

CUTTING ROOM FLOOR - GETTING TO THE "ONE" THING!

| 25 Backlog Items | 5 Backlog Items | Top 1 thing |

- – To Do Items

With 25 items, to focus on all 25 would require that you split your attention between them, resulting in less that 4% of your attention on each one. Already cutting it to five items increases your productivity 5-fold and you could devote 20% of your attention to each one. Bringing it down to one gives you a chance to give your full attention to your "one thing."

Simple? Yes. Easy to do? No.

In the Cascading Vision image at the beginning of this chapter, we depict a series of dominoes on the left side, where each successive domino grows in size by 50%. If you start with a 2-inch domino, the second domino would be 3 inches tall. The third domino would be 4.5 inches tall, and so on. Gary Keller captures this geometric progression in his book "The One Thing." In our example, we will only look at the progression up through the 19th Domino:

GEOMETRIC PROGRESSION WHERE
EACH SUCCESSIVE DOMINO INCREASES BY 50%
AND YOU BEGIN WITH A 2 INCH DOMINO...
BY THE 19TH DOMINO, IT IS 246 FEET TALL!
(TALLER THAN THE LEANING TOWER OF PISA)

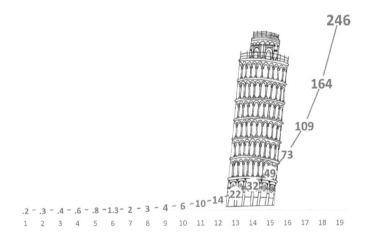

This demonstrates the powerful impact of small actions that are continuously focused on the Right People Vision, the clear "one" thing.

At the 19th domino, the size of the domino is taller than the Leaning Tower of Pisa. At 25 dominos, it's as tall as the Eiffel Tower. At 31 it's taller than Mount Everest. And, at 57 you've almost made it to the moon!

There is a video on YouTube that visualizes using dominoes as a metaphor at the following link: https://www.youtube.com/watch?v=aqJdtc7CvtM

One of the biggest blockers for the Vision ("one thing") to freely flow, domino-to-domino throughout the organization, is language. The language spoken at the Executive, Senior Management (i.e. Portfolio level) and Program Levels seldom has anything to do with the language spoken by the Project, Team or Individual levels.

The result is a dilution of focus, and thus the Vision, which eliminates the power of the domino effect. This can also result in a disconnect between the levels. It's the difference between the Language of Leadership and the Language of Management.

What is most powerful in any organization is the ability to effectively and accurately transmit the Vision throughout all team level and individual activities. And, linking back the "one thing" from the individual and team levels back up through the organization has the potential to create exponential value-add.

And when you factor in the fact that the Business and IT/Tech sides of the organization also have their own "languages," it becomes clear that having clear Definitions, to which everyone agrees (i.e. Distillation) is the only way to insure Delivering value and Driving the organization forward.

In the past, we have used the 1 Language + 1 Mind + 1 Plan = 1 Vision formula to communicate the need for this clarity. The dominoes Mr. Keller used in the example in his book are the clearest visual of how this works that we have ever seen.

Additionally, we created the Vision Flow Formula to help organizations visualize the negative results of poorly Defined and/or communicated Vision:

Flow = Vision + Right People + 4D Model
*4D Model = Define (**D1**) → Distill (**D2**) →*
*Deliver (**D3**) → Drive (**D4**)*

■■■■■■ + RP + D1 + D2 + D3 + D4 = Anarchy

Vision + ■■ + D1 + D2 + D3 + D4 = Anxiety

Vision + RP + ■■ + D2 + D3 + D4 = Confusion

Vision + RP + D1 + ■■ + D3 + D4 = Politics

Vision + RP + D1 + D2 + ■■ + D4 = Chaos

Vision + RP + D1 + D2 + D3 + ■■ = Division

If the Vision is poorly Defined (or, even missing), then the probability of having Anarchy in the organization is high. If you have the wrong people in the wrong roles, then Anxiety among your team members will probably go through the roof. Any part of the 4D Model that is missing will most likely result in Confusion, Politic, Chaos and/or Division. The word "Division," by the way, in English literally means "two Visions." United we stand and divided we fall.

And, Distillation to the "one thing" at every level will insure exponential results. For the SingTel case study, we began from the point we entered; at the team, product and project levels.

- ☐ What is the Vision for the team?
- ☐ What is the value-add that we are going to Deliver?
- ☐ Why are we doing this?
- ☐ How does the team's Vision link to the Vision of the product, service or result that we are trying to achieve?
- ☐ How does the team's Vision link to the program(s), process(es) and portfolio(s) to which it belongs?

☐ How does the team Vision link back to the top-line Purpose, Mission and Vision of the organization?

If the top-level Vision, Mission and Purpose are ponderous, dense, multiple or unclear it is even worse. Without clarity, most organizational Vision statements do not inform an individual's work at the task level. Also, even fewer organizations are able to create an effective feedback loop from the bottom-up, which when properly functioning creates an exponential 2" domino effect. Each task becomes focused on the Delivery of the Vision.

This is further illustrated by David Marquet in his book "Turn the Ship Around":

"Connecting our day-to-day activities to something larger was a strong motivator for the crew. The connection was there but it had been lost. Instead, in ways large and small, I encountered situations where the crew's actions were motivated by following a checklist, pleasing an inspector, looking good, or some other variant of 'avoiding problems.' I, we, needed everyone to see the ultimate purpose for the submarine and remember that it was a noble purpose. I also wanted to connect out current endeavors with the submarine force's rich legacy of service to and sacrifice for the country. Once the crewman remembered what we were doing and why, they would do anything to support the mission. This was a stark contrast to earlier, when people were coming to work simply with the hope of not screwing up."[26]

He Cascaded his VSPT creating a high-performing culture! If the Vision is not simple and clear, the individuals and teams will not be able to respond in Delivering the Vision. If the teams and individuals are not Delivering on the Vision, then communicating clearly back to the next levels above via the feedback loops will be broken, non-existent or blocked.

"As one senior leader from Whole Foods put it, "We don't think about growing the brand—that's MBA talk. We're about fulfilling our mission."[27]

GARY HAMEL

Having successful feedback loops provides useful information and trends with which the executive leadership can make valuable, sustainable and beneficial decisions for the organization. VSPT (Vision, Strategy, People and Tasks), as shown in the graphic above, should occur at every level in the organization and needs to be Defined by the leaders, teams and individuals at each and every level.

The feedback loops, in both directions, in a high-functioning Cascade, will relate to the "why" and in some respects the "what," but not necessarily the "how:"

"In most organizations, control is exercised via standard operating procedures, tight supervision, detail role definitions, a minimum of self-directed time, and frequent reviews by higher-ups. These mechanisms certainly bring people to heel, but they also put a short leash on initiative, creativity, and passion. Luckily there are other ways of keeping things in check—other "hows," if you will." [28]

We shared an example of this other type of "how" in our book, "The Nehemiah Effect":

"By following this process you gain alignment, or unity, from the individuals performing tasks to the re-prioritization of strategic initiatives by the executive team and it is clear up and down the organizational chart how it all fits together.

An example of how this can function effectively is the work we did with Bethany Christian Services, the largest adoption agency in the world with 1,500 employees in 90 locations. Bethany's vision Statement states "We envision a world where every child is in a loving home." As we worked with the various functional teams within Bethany to create cascading purpose, mission and vision statements the development team result truly stands out.

In the Non-Profit world, the Development group is the fund-raising team. Thus, you would think that the mission, or business that they are in, would be related to raising money to fuel the organization needs and goals. The Mission statement created by the team stated; "Connecting Resources to Vulnerable Children." Succinct, elegant and right on the mark for what they are trying to do as a team.

The vision statement, what they want to be, was equally good; "To Model and Inspire Exceptional Giving." As a team, they felt that they needed to be models of the type of giving they were asking donors to participate in. This in turn would generate results because their work effort would spring from the reality they are living and modeling. We trust you see how this allows the functional area to live the

Organizational Vision within the context of what they are tasked to Deliver in their function.

Thus, a cascading vision that is different from the main vision feeds the 'why' of the functional areas with the core meaning of the true vision of the enterprise.

We then create a purpose, mission and vision statement for each project. It has to capture in a short phrase how this project will fulfill the purpose, mission and vision of the team and the functional area and the entire company. All of the vision statements are listed in the project charter and the project mission and vision statements are in the header for all project documents, so that the team is continually reminded why they are delivering on the tasks they are working on." [29]

In addition, VSPT and the "one" thing as Cascading dominoes (focused on the most important action) are the iterative links between the various levels as you go back up the left side of the figure above. This is the most powerful feature of Cascading the Vision. When that link is done properly, it provides the vital feedback loop back up the food chain that enables the organization to adapt and adjust to the rapidly changing marketplace battlefield.

Without this feedback loop it risks being nothing more than business as usual with upper management feeling that they have effectively communicated the Vision. But, when they don't see the results they were looking for, they end up micromanaging the teams at the task level.

Focusing on details should not be confused with micromanaging. Those are two different things. Focusing on small steps, in the right direction, to accomplish large things is great advice regardless of your product or business.

"Great things are done by a series of small things brought together." [30]
VINCENT VAN GOGH

However, there is no worse mistake that an enterprise can make than to give too much "direction" (i.e. legacy Command and Control) from the top. It creates an atmosphere that smothers creativity and kills Flow. Daniel Pink sums it up this way:

"Control leads to compliance; autonomy leads to engagement." [31]

Gallup, in its most recent survey regarding engagement, shows the engagement level for managers is at 35%. Here are some quotes from two articles about engagement at Gallup.com:

"Day in and day out, managers are tasked with engaging employees, but 51% of managers have essentially "checked out," meaning they care little, if at all, about their job and company. And that attitude has dire consequences. A manager's engagement -- or lack thereof -- affects his or her employees' engagement, creating what Gallup calls the cascade effect." [32]

"While economic conditions can help explain employee engagement readings to some degree, Gallup has found that engagement is tied to many factors—managers being chief among them. Gallup research shows that a manager's engagement – or lack thereof – affects his or her employees' engagement, creating a cascade effect. Essentially, employees' engagement is directly influenced by their managers' engagement whose engagement is directly influenced by their manager's engagement." [33]

"Managers have the greatest impact on employee engagement, which makes this finding very worrisome: A strikingly low percentage -- just 35% -- of U.S. managers are themselves engaged, while 51% are not engaged and 14% are actively disengaged." [34]

"By Gallup's estimates, the "not engaged" group costs the U.S. $77 billion to $96 billion annually through their impact on those they manage. And when we factor in the impact of the "actively disengaged" group, those figures jump to $319 billion to $398 billion annually." [35]

The line that we draw between the VS (Vision and Strategy) and PT (People and Tasks) in the image below is how we communicate the disconnect that the Gallup findings demonstrate:

V
S

P
T

We have found this disconnect to be true in almost every company with which we've worked. VSPT is also the first and most important Definition that should be completed.

In other words, before you can create a Definition of "done" the work on creating a clear Vision and the "one" thing needs to be finished. Each team, starting at the board level and executive teams down to the implementation team level must Define their VSPT and "one" thing.

Not doing the necessary work to simplify and eliminate complexity costs even more as Gallup estimated above. Ignoring the problem doesn't magically make it go away. Assuming that it is done is even worse.

The value-add of engaged simplification is stunning. Many times, as demonstrated by our SingTel story, it can be realized quickly and the results can even seem magical.

The more complex the organization is, the more opportunity exists to simplify. It's starts with Cascading Vision from the very top of the organization on downwards and then linking back up from each level so that there is a feedback loop that helps adjust and shape the big Vision over time. This is what we call Vision Flow. Captain David Marquet has an elegant description of how this works:

"We discovered that distributing control by itself wasn't enough. As that happened, it put requirements on the new decision makers to have a higher level of technical knowledge and clearer sense of organizational purpose than ever before. That's because decisions are made against a set of criteria that includes what's technically appropriate and what aligns with the organization's interests." [36]

By the way, our usage of VSPT is a modification of the West Point military strategic approach that uses "Vision, Strategy, *Projects* and *Tactics*" as a part of its leadership framework.

In our experience, the "P" can stand for portfolios, products, programs, projects, etc. But, we have chosen People for the P in our VSPT because the individual is vital and key to the success of the Enterprise at every level. In the end, it all boils down to People and the Tasks on which they are working and that is why we changed the "T" to Tasks in our version. How you structure the organization and its functional workflow is secondary. It is vital to have the Right People on the bus. And, most importantly, team members that shouldn't be on the bus need to be invited to explore better fitting opportunities or find a different bus. This is particularly true if the individual is toxic.

Either way, VSPT is a simple and powerful method to link and align all teams and people to the overall Vision of the organization and make sure that they are engaged in the Right People Flow.

The first step in making any move to a Flow environment is to understand that a change needs to be made. The enterprise needs to have a clear Vision of why, when and how they are going to attain Flow. If this is not simple and clear, then work remains to be done. Don't stop honing and refining. Continue working until the Vision is truly simple, clean and understandable; and, you have identified the "one" thing.

The Vision "intent" for your company needs to be clear and concise (this is the similar idea to military document called the "commander's intent"). Not more than five to seven words long. Your Vision statement needs to be memorable and easy to communicate, so anything longer than seven words will in most cases become unwieldy and not memorable.

When the Purpose, Vision and Mission statements are too long, then entering into and maintaining Flow becomes difficult, if not impossible. Vision needs to be communicated much more often and effectively than we think or realize. It needs to be central to everything that the teams are doing. It needs to be checked daily, if not continuously. As we stated in Nehemiah Effect:

"If you are not governed by vision, then you will be tossed about on the stormy waters of circumstance. For most businesses, the color of the ocean doesn't matter if you're in the middle of a hurricane." [37]

IF YOU ARE NOT LED BY VISION, YOU WILL BE DRIVEN BY CIRCUMSTANCE.

A culture of Vision, implemented correctly, simplifies everything and helps the organization flow properly. Everything that is important is measured against it. Everything else is waste and can be brutally eliminated. It crystalizes the focus of the enterprise with laser-like precision and unnecessary or unneeded features and activities are eliminated. They never see the light of day.

True Vision, properly constructed, does not adapt and adjust. How you get to it does. Do the necessary work and stay focused. Know your "one" thing and Deliver it.

By the way, an excellent book on maintaining product focus using the principles we describe as Cascading Vision and VSPT is "User Story Mapping: Discover the Whole Story, Build the Right Product" by Jeff Patton.

Prioritize

Jim Collins and William Lazier, in their book "Beyond Entrepreneurship" that was published in 1992 (long before the Agile Manifesto was written), understood that if a team is failing to Deliver then management needs to look in the mirror for the problem:

"...a central tenet of tactical excellence: if your people aren't executing well, it's not their fault. It's yours." [38]

People can't execute well or Deliver consistent, sustainable results if they don't know or understand the highest priority on which they should direct their effort. Our Cascading VSPT and One Language + One Mind + One Plan formula have accomplished this for us for a very long time. We recently added a twist, via Gary

Keller, founder of Keller-Williams Real Estate, the largest real estate firm in the world. He describes how he focused his organization with a Cascading VSPT effect that he labels the "one thing." It is a process of continuous Distillation from the highest level down to the individual task, which constantly focuses on the highest priority. The single most important part of this process is a question he developed and then asked himself, and everyone in his organization, over and over and over again. They still use it today:

"What's the ONE Thing you can do this week such that by doing it everything else would be easier or unnecessary?"

Keller-Williams has grown 40% per year every year since initiating this question over 20 years ago.

The laser focus created by continuously asking this question can cause any organization to obtain exponential results, regardless of underlying management methodologies. It does require executive buy-in and leadership, which Keller delivered to his organization. He is a rare exception.

A vacuum of this type of understanding by the leadership is one of the main reasons scaling Agile has been difficult for so many organizations around the world.

The Board and Executive Level Octagon (Creating the Cage Fight)

"Top managers frequently look at project budgets as a cost, not an investment, and see project activities as part of operations. They rarely appoint a 'chief project officer' or vice president of projects, and their project teams are left on their own with little guidance or help from the top." [39]

AARON SHENHAR AND DOV DVIR

Much of our work over the past decade has been directed at the creation and optimization of program management offices (PMOs) in Europe, the US and Asia. As a result, we have observed the difficulties encountered when companies try to scale Agile (a very effective group of team-level practices that facilitate Flow and High-Performance) to the Enterprise level. In recent years, it has become clear that there is a massive gap between Agile teams and organizational leadership in almost every customer's situation. For the past two decades, we have pictured this gap using VSPT (Vision, Strategy, People and Tasks) as we shared in the image earlier.

Every time we have used this graphic in training or consulting situations, we get universal agreement that the gap is real, significant and exists in their organizations.

It comes as no surprise that team-level Scrum and Agile, as frameworks or methodologies, do not address or cure this disconnect. Scrum and most Agile methods are optimized for the team level. Yes, the values in the Agile Manifesto may (or may not) scale to an organization, but the manifesto limits itself, by Definition, to only software development and the focus is on improving team level performance, not the entire organization (or, for example, beyond IT).

The gap occurs, in large part, because executive leadership uses different language than rest of the organization:

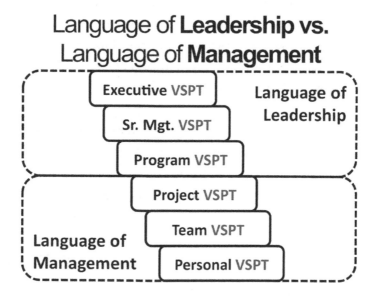

Agile tools and methods are effective at the team level. There are tools and methods aimed at bridging parts of this organizational gap (i.e. SAFe, Management 3.0, LeSS, Enterprise Scrum, DAD, etc.). But, all of these attempts are still dependent on team-level methodologies and constraints. For example, SAFe is predicated upon having all of the development and operational teams successfully using Scrum. Not all organizations have the discipline or maturity to do so. This can lead to a strong need for extensive and expensive customization, thus losing much of the expected benefit. All of these tools are methods that focus on process and rules. However, scaling team-success organizationally requires passion and Purpose:

"(Elon) Musk, like every entrepreneur...is driven by passion and purpose. Why? Passion and purpose scale---always have, always will. Every movement, every revolution, is proof of this fact." [40]

Flow identifies and maintains organizational focus on the white-hot why, which helps successfully bridge all the disconnects.

For example, at Nature Publishing Group (NPG), when Andrew was there leading the Waterfall to Agile transformation, part of the equation included putting in place an Agile PMO (Program and Portfolio Management Office). But, we quickly learned at NPG that an Agile PMO wasn't enough to complete the transformation. We found that we also needed an Agile Transformation Group (ATG) to help champion the massive changes we were implementing throughout the organization. Without something akin to an Agile Transformation Group, led from the highest level, the hierarchy and its tribal powers remain intact.

> *"Hierarchies are very good at aggregating effort, at coordinating the activities of many people with widely varying roles. But they're not very good at mobilizing effort – at inspiring people to go above and beyond. When it comes to mobilizing, human capability, communities outperform bureaucracies... in a bureaucracy you are a factor of production. In a community you are a partner in a cause."* [41]
>
> **GARY HAMEL**

Project Management Offices tend to be rather bureaucratic. A properly constructed and functioning ATG is a community of peers focused on Delivering the Vision. You need a proper balance of both of these to be successful. It is basically creating a high-functioning community even in a highly structured command-and-control hierarchy. Gary Hamel quotes Bill Gore, founder of W. L. Gore and Associates (i.e. Gore-Tex, etc.) who believed:

"In every organization there (is) an informal matrix of relationships underlying what he called 'the façade of authoritarian hierarchy.' His goal: get rid of the façade." [42]

The ATG at NPG consisted of senior executives. It included Technology's Portfolio Manager (Andrew), the Head of Platforms, the Head of Product Management, the Head of Project Management (including the two senior managers in charge of all of the ScrumMasters/Project Managers), and the Head of Software Development.

Some of the key items that the ATG Delivered were:

☐ The agreed upon Definition for "NPG Agile"
☐ Sorting all of the development teams into persistent (dedicated) teams
☐ Handling of exceptions
☐ Communication with the Board and C-level
☐ Normalizing Agile between the various offices and countries involved

The above list can look deceptively simple. Getting those items done in an organization that had a legacy of a command-and-control culture took the ATG over 1.5 years to complete.

This is why an ATG can be similar to a no-holds-barred "cage fight" in the octagon. For those that are not familiar with the octagon, it is the shape of the ring in which combatants do battle in some fight environments. Distilling agreement, at times, can look more like a smack down in a cage fight rather than an ad hoc committee meeting of executives.

Without first Distilling agreement, it is not possible to create a "safe" space for teams to navigate the stormy waters that Distillation causes. It takes firm yet flexible leadership to maintain a consistent Vision for change.

During the transition time frame, the NPG PMO Delivered the following key items:

☐ Training 250 team members and stakeholders in "NPG Agile" during a 12-month period
☐ Facilitated the forced-prioritization of the project pipeline from 250 down to 100

- ☐ The baseline of project completion performance was 60 projects per year at the beginning of 2011
- ☐ By 2013 the newly trained "NPG Agile" teams were able to Deliver 124 projects per year, more than doubling productivity while reducing headcount by 10%
- ☐ Increased Communication, Reporting and Transparency with the ATG, Board and C-level

The NPG PMO also developed standards, templates, etc. But, for example, we eliminated the use of full-blown, up-front business cases for almost all projects. The original NPG "template" for a business case was 12 pages long and once filled-in could be as much as 50 pages. For over 80% of all projects we substituted a one-page business case from which the executives could make quick decisions. This is one reason for the increased throughput.

Both the PMO and ATG members were also actively involved in the budgetary process, but we found that once we dedicated the teams they became a fixed cost. As a publisher, we were also dealing with fixed deadlines as well, so the only variable became scope. When it became clear (via our reporting structure) that a team was not going to be able to Deliver the minimum viable product by the due date, then the executives were, once again, forced to reprioritize the project backlog.

This early warning radar worked really well for the executives. For example, one time we had a product manager (and the Product Owner reporting to her) that kept communicating to the ATG, the executives and the board that a key project would be Delivered in April. The team doing the work kept reporting back to the PMO that this wasn't the case. Once we pinpointed the cause of the disagreement, it was clear that the Product Owner had miscalculated the actual time necessary to complete the project by a factor of two.

The estimates and reports were corrected and the PMO communicated the new Delivery date of July/August back to the ATG, C-level and Board. Once the Board and executives got over the initial shock, they realized that they had just been warned of a problem 4 to 5 months earlier than normal, if they had been still using the old system. That resulted in major cost avoidance and savings. It also allowed time for adjustments to be made in advance, rather than dealing with a fire drill once the deadline was missed.

So, we have found that using Flow, an ATG plus an Agile PMO are superb governance tools for scaling Agile team success to the enterprise level.

But, what about companies that began in an Agile fashion or that consider themselves fully transformed to Agile? Do they need Flow, an ATG and an Agile PMO?

Yes.

In those situations, they will still need the elements of Flow, an ATG and an Agile PMO. This will help them maintain discipline, continue to mature and fully scale Agile to the Enterprise level.

Of course, this assumes that the organization's program and portfolio management (PPM) have already begun operating in Flow. If not, then there is quite a bit of work to do on two fronts, instead of one. A ponderous, tools and rules-based PPM or PMO has killed off more than a few high-performing Agile teams.

By the way, in our experience, Scrum of Scrums isn't a viable substitute for Agile governance. At best, it is a tool used within an Agile environment that can be helpful and used to synchronize a number of teams working on the same product, project and/or program.

There are other more powerful tools, like quarterly walkabout workshops (i.e. "big room" or release planning), that can be used at the program and portfolio levels to help capture and create transparency. This kind of workshop helps to smoke out cross-dependencies and integration items that extend outside of a multi-team project (i.e. items that cut across multiple departments, tribes, guilds, programs and portfolios). For more on this topic, see our blog post at https://pmobrothers.wordpress.com/2015/02/19/how-to-get-started-with-agile-governance-19-feb-2015/.

We have also seen entrepreneurial start-up companies (that were Agile from the start) have difficulty maintaining high-performance once they got to a certain size. It is somewhere between the 700 to 1,000-person range that the ability of the organization to organically manage itself is outstripped by growth. At this point in time "team Agile" stops working. A different approach is needed.

A Flow structure facilitates the transition from being entrepreneurial to a more mature business. Flow is even more powerful when used right from the start.

One significant mistake that some companies are making is trying to use agile coaching methodologies from the team level to scale agile to the enterprise level. To be fair, some agile coaches may have the skill, experience and ability to assist an organization making the transition. However, we have observed that most agile coaches are not able to successfully help migrate team success to overall enterprise success. It is not a native skill set.

Visibility

Jim Collins in "Beyond Entrepreneurship," also talks about the importance of keeping your Vision visible at all times. Here's how he states it:

"Once you have your vision and strategy, it's necessary to translate them into solid, tactical execution. The first step is to make sure that all key people have a copy of the vision, strategy and current year's strategic priorities in front of them at all times. They should be brought to every staff meeting. They should be referred to constantly." [43]

With the rise of tools like JIRA, Rally, VersionOne, ScrumWise, etc. in Agile environments, we have observed an interesting phenomenon: if the teams do not take time to actually do the work to create a physical Scrum or Kanban board (either with post-it notes or the backlog items directly printed out from JIRA and then pasted to a physical board) then backlog items can be missed and/ or completely forgotten. Out of sight equals out of mind. This happened time and time again on the projects at NPG. Some of the teams were complaining about having to do "duplicate" work. But, when they actually took the extra time needed to make the work effort big and visible, almost without exception they discovered items that they had completely missed. And, without those items in the workflow or sprint (a sprint is a specific time box on one to two weeks used to shorten Delivery times in Agile projects), they would have failed to Deliver the full value that could be realized by including all of the items in the sprint backlog. By forcing visibility, we eliminated error and rework for the teams and the projects and increased the quality of the end result Delivered.

Collins and Lazier describe an effective utilization of this principle:

"In watching Doug Stone, former CEO of Personal CAD Systems, move about the company, we noticed that he drew pictures of the company's strategy on flip charts, in offices and conference rooms throughout the building. During nearly every meeting he somehow got around to drawing the diagrams, and he left these little drawings all over: on scraps of paper, on people's notepads, on flip charts, on white boards, on bulletin boards, on lunchroom napkins. When asked about this, he said: 'I leave those drawings around on purpose. It's really hard to get an entire organization to understand where it's going, so you've got to keep hammering at the message. I leave those drawings around so that people will continually bump into them and perhaps refer to them during meetings. I guess it's kind of like subliminal suggestion.'" [44]

Not only should the Vision and the work effort be visible and ubiquitous, the successful progress towards the overall Vision should be appropriately consolidated and reported to all stakeholders. One of the principles of Agile is "transparency," but it is a fascinating irony that many times it feels like Agile "purists" don't want to be measured in any way, under any circumstances and at any time. However, velocity alone (team, program, portfolio or organizational) is not enough. But, it is a step in the right direction. Keeping the Vision and velocity of all teams visible increases transparency and accountability.

In a recent presentation shared by Rally Software in May, 2014 in Stockholm, Sweden, they pointed out that, on average, user stories tend to end up the same size. This data was collected from over 13,000 teams and/or companies that are using Rally's software. At NPG, the same phenomenon was observed. It didn't matter if the company used hours or points, the relative size of the work effort and the team level ends up being roughly the same. While many of us in the Agile community had anecdotal evidence and a strong gut feeling about sizing work effort, Rally nailed it with their research.

Mentioning anything that even sounds like key performance indicators (KPIs) usually sends Agile enthusiasts running for the door. What they fail to realize is that they need team KPIs to be able to communicate up the food chain to senior management, executives, the C-level and the Board in a way that is simple to understand and that can be tracked over a longer period of time.

Sprint burndown (or burnup) charts are a useful Agile KPI tool and we agree that these are useful tools at the team level. And, it is a fact that they can be (and are) often misused by well-intentioned (or not so well-intentioned) managers that try to reverse engineer who is individually underperforming. In other words, with data, the beatings will continue until morale improves. Having seen the negative impacts of this anti-pattern, we only encourage team-level reporting by teams for self-improvement. For the most part the burn-up charts should be off-limits to management if they have not been properly trained in Flow.

Release Burnup charts become useful after four to six successful sprints. At this point we can begin to project when the team will be able to Deliver something akin to the minimum viable product (MVP). This can make teams nervous because they feel like they are committing to Delivering the whole product backlog. That is not the case nor the intent.

The beauty of Agile is that it allows the Product Owner the opportunity to reprioritize the backlog before the next sprint starts, so that the highest value user stories (product backlog items, work packages, requirements, activities, tasks, etc.) are included in the next iteration. We additionally make sure to communicate that the team is NOT promising to Deliver the whole backlog, but rather the specific part of the backlog that will add the most immediate value to the company. This does not preclude the use of team velocity data for future planning purposes. It just keeps the team focused on the appropriate "2-inch" domino.

As companies start to get the hang of working with Epics and Themes (portfolio-level user stories) and Features (program or product-level capabilities, usually captured in the form of a sub-epic or user story), those individuals that are working at the PMO and portfolio levels of an organization have a new way to measure and communicate trends that have meaning for executives. Using Vision as the ultimate Epic or Theme allows the Product Backlog to encompass the appropriate work effort needed to Deliver the Vision. Also, all acceptance criteria will thus reflect the True Vision.

Whatever methodology that is used to Deliver the Vision, it should be customized to match an organization's culture, governance structure and reporting needs. These data and trends can be used to make better decisions. For example, as you will see in the NPG case study in Appendix A, at the beginning of NPG's Agile transformation there was only a 1-in-4 chance that the right projects would be done during the next 12 months. This situation was the result of the team's then current velocity of 60 completed projects per year with a total backlog of 250. If you guessed incorrectly or had self-prioritized a lower-value project on which to focus, then the organizational return-on-investment was potentially diminished or eliminated.

Short Cycles

"We live in an uncertain world. We must recognize that our original plan was based on noisy data, viewed from a long-time horizon." [45]

DONALD REINERTSEN

"…cadence helps to control the progressive accumulation of the variability in the development processes. Today's orthodoxy constrains the scope of work and drives variability into timing. The new paradigm constrains timing and drives variability into the scope of work. These two approaches are fundamentally different … the more detail we made our plans, the longer our cycle times became. We favor highly granular planning because we don't understand the statistics of variability. Misunderstanding variability is dangerous in the repetitive world of manufacturing, but it is even more dangerous in product development where variability is much higher." [46]

DONALD REINERTSEN

The problem and paradox faced by almost all PMOs is the ability to forecast and estimate when projects and/or products will be Delivered. The primary reason for this is that teams are not able to effectively forecast beyond the next 90-days. So, if you have a roadmap that stretches out over one or two years, then you need to factor in significant variability and change to the scope or timelines.

So, from the PMO level and up in an organization, the need for Flow increases exponentially.

"…today's product development orthodoxy tends to use centralized control. We create project management offices (PMOs). We create centralized information systems. We centralize buffers to take advantage of the efficiency

This centralized, control style of thinking, limits quick adaptation and team innovation. For example, at NPG they had aggressive Goals to increase traffic, registrations and subscriptions generated by their website. None of the executives actually believed that the numbers could be achieved within a one-year period of time since they had never performed at that level previously. But, this was two years into the Agile transformation. So, when they brought the new projects to the development organization, which would, if successful, enable them to achieve the hoped-for level of high-performance, the teams were able to quickly pivot and Deliver what the executives needed. Within nine months, all of the Goals were surpassed. Notice, the new projects were not added to the planned work effort of the teams. A reprioritization occurred and some projects were delayed, so the new projects could be Delivered.

"The current orthodoxy does not focus on understanding deeper economic relationships. Instead, it is, at best, based on observing correlations between pairs of proxy variables. For example, it observes that late design changes have higher costs than early design changes, and prescribes front-loading problem solving. This ignores the fact that late changes can also create enormous economic value. The economic effect of a late change can only be evaluated by considering its complete economic impact." [48]

DONALD REINERTSEN

A perfect example of what Reinertsen is describing above is the completed Sydney Opera house project that was a decade late and over $100 million over budget with vastly expanded scope. But, the overall result was in the billions per year in direct value that is continuously added to the Australian economy.

Rob Flaherty in a March 2014 blog post shared these insights into Reinertsen's Definition and use of Proxy Variables:

"A few pages into The Principles of Product Development Flow, Donald Reinertsen brings up the notion of proxy variables and provides this definition: "A proxy variable is a quantified measure that substitutes for the real economic objective: life-cycle profits." He goes on to say, "By focusing on proxy variables, product developers delude themselves into thinking they understand their economics. They do not." And finally, "It's only when we understand the mapping between proxy variables and life-cycle profits that we can really see the economic consequences of our choices."" [49]

The Proxy Variables are a deep problem in almost every organization with which we have worked. There is not space in this book to address this topic thoroughly. But its relevance cannot be understated.

The importance of the mathematical proofs in Reinertsen's book are the identification and Definition of the difference between a proxy variable and a true variable. If you optimize a proxy variable without considering the Vision impacts on the true variable, then you are delivering the wrong thing. The Vision should Define the true variable and all adjustments to proxy variables.

We have experienced and taught that operating using short cycles, continuous reprioritization against new learnings and adaption to changing environments mitigates any concerns about "late changes." They become irrelevant.

Optimizing using Flow does not mean that queues are eliminated. Rather, it means that the highest value-add of the entire work stream is balanced against available capacity and the cost associated with any individual queue.

This requires Vision to work.

Unless the value of the desired product, service or result is constructed by and measured against the Vision, then no one knows why they are doing what they are doing. The risk this creates is enormous. They risk focusing on the wrong, inappropriate or self-prioritized thing at the queuing points while missing the over-arching Vision. In essence, you are starting a domino Cascade that could become exponential in its effect, but in the wrong direction.

A great example is the Vietnam War. According to Harry G. Summers in his book "On Strategy" as quoted by Collins and Lazier, although the US Army efficiently moved over 1 million soldiers a year to and from Vietnam and supported them logistically better than any conflict in history, the US still lost the war.

Why?

"A 1974 survey of Army Generals who had commanded in Vietnam found that almost 70% of them were uncertain of United States objectives ... 'this confusion over objectives,' Summers concluded, 'had a devastating effect on the United States ability to conduct the war.'" [50]

If you don't have a clear Vision or know the "why," then an efficient "how" really doesn't matter. You will still end up losing.

A good example of this comes from the Agile community. An Agile "purist" is a person that believes that their Agile "method" is the only way to get things done properly and that all other methodologies are, by tribal practice, inferior. They have not come far enough up the learning curve to truly look for new and better ways to do things and in doing so, they have missed the whole point of the Agile Manifesto. Agile purists that operate in this way make the same mistake the Generals did in the Vietnam war. With religious zeal, they "hold a space for Scrum (Kanban, XP, etc.)" just for the sake of being "unpolluted" in their approach as it relates to the tribal rules. That is, they are focused on team or Scrum efficiency. But, they neglect the bigger picture.

The reality is that we need to hold a space for the True Vision of the organization (i.e. the big picture and/or "one thing") and not let anything detract from that. We are not saying that the rules of any particular methodology have no value; we are saying that we value the True Vision more. Don't let Proxy Variables divert you from True Variables.

Intrinsic Motivation and Transformation

"Workers throughout history could be 'supervised.' They could be told what to do, how to do it, how fast to do it and so on. Knowledge workers cannot, in effect, be supervised." [51]

PETER DRUCKER

We hope that by now we have effectively communicated the importance of using Vision as the Driver to lead organizational change management or to reshape a culture. Simon Cinek actually nailed it on the head in his book, "Start with WHY" where he shared:

"I trust my gut ... it's a good strategy, except it's not scalable. The gut decision can only be made by a single person. It's a perfectly good strategy for an individual or a small organization, but what happens when success necessitates that more people be able to make decisions that 'feel' right? That's when the power of WHY can be fully realized. The ability to put a WHY into words provides the emotional context for decisions." [52]

Bingo!

At a recent Global Leadership Summit webcast for the Swedish-speaking executives and leaders in the Jakobstad, Finland area (13 - 14 November 2015), Bill Hybels took Cinek's idea of "WHY" and enhanced it to:

"You must find your white hot WHY and live it out with your entire heart!" [53]

While this scales easily to both the individual and team levels, it remains a challenge at the program, portfolio and enterprise levels. This is also why the success of "team level" Agile is so difficult to scale to the rest of the organization. Models and methods that facilitate excellent intrinsic motivation at the team and individual level are not necessarily well suited for use at the enterprise level.

We have found that the four lenses on transformation is a simple 4-box that can be used to quickly assess each key area in an organization:

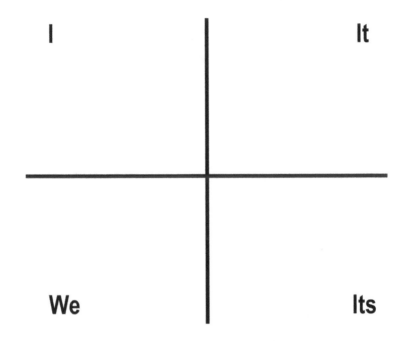

This format was shared at the Scrum Gathering Las Vegas (SGLAS 2013) where Andrew had the opportunity to participate in a workshop facilitated by Lyssa Adkins and Michael Spayd on the Windows on Transformation: Four Pathways to Grow a More Agile Enterprise (the **I, We, It and It's** 4-box applied to Scrum and Agile).

We love this box as a visual structure to help explain where and how to communicate Vision throughout an organization. However, the circumstance or physical environment of your organization may limit the use of visual tools. If this is your situation, you will need to get creative, but it still remains important to Cascade the Vision and the "one thing" for each quadrant.

If visual props are not possible, then verbal tools can be effectively substituted. For example, Captain Marquet shares an incredible example of verbally painting the Vision he used for the transformation of his crew:

"Connecting our day-to-day activities to something larger was a strong motivator for the crew. The connection was there but it had been lost. Instead, in ways large and small, I encountered situations where the crew's actions were motivated by following a checklist, pleasing an inspector, looking good, or some other variant of 'avoiding

problems.' I, we, needed everyone to see the ultimate purpose for the submarine and remember that it was a noble purpose. I also wanted to connect our current endeavors with the submarine force's rich legacy of service to and sacrifice for country. Once the crewmen remembered what we were doing and why, they would do anything to support the mission." [54]

What Captain Marquet did was to intuitively and orally use the "I, We, It and Its" four-box to keep Vision foremost in the minds of his team members. This is a simple framework, and as you already know, we like simple.

After the workshop with Lyssa and Michael, Andrew created the following graphic to show how the UVF and Flow can be used to Deliver remarkable results and positive change in all four boxes:

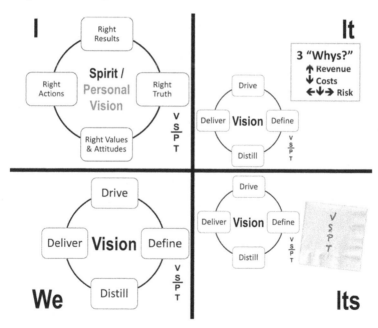

Lyssa and Michael's workshop did a great job outlining the "who" and the "what" for Agile transformation. Flow and the Unified Vision Framework actually Deliver the "how" to actually implement a transformation, as shown above.

There are additional items that they addressed in all four areas above, but what they presented at that Scrum Gathering didn't communicate to the participants a crisp understanding of "how" to implement in each of the 4 areas. They have since updated their slides to reflect what Andrew shared with them right after the conference. [55]

While on the surface it would make sense, and appear that teams should be able to organically scale using "team" Agile (from the **We** quadrant), the reality for most companies, even for those that started out Agile, is quite the opposite.

There are organizational dynamics that "team Agile" is not equipped to manage, nor should it try. See our blog post Agile Can't Scale: Fact or Myth (https://pmobrothers.wordpress.com/) for a more detailed discussion.

The UVF and Flow bridge this gap.

It is powerful because Flow continuously and iteratively communicates and focuses the Vision in all four boxes and keeps it aligned at all organizational levels. Flow is deceptively simple and effective. It breaks through the tribal barriers and gets everyone on the same page. Remember, if you make any changes in one quadrant, it automatically impacts and changes the other three.

Frameworks by themselves, however effective, don't implement themselves. Here is how we applied the four quadrants at SingTel:

Individual transformation

In the case studies in Appendix A we use the following Vision Flow checklist to determine the "health" of a project. Here's what the assignment at SingTel looked like:

> ### THEY HAD THE FOLLOWING CHALLENGES:
> x Anarchy
> x Anxiety
> x Confusion
> x Politics
> x Chaos
> x Division

Combining the Vision Flow checklist with the "I, We, It, Its" 4-box is a quick and powerful way to do a root cause or current state analysis; and, from that create the fastest path from "as is" to the "to be" state of organizational Flow. Here is an expanded version of the 4-box for explaining the SingTel project.

"I" (Individual) lens

In this window at SingTel we used both the 4R Model – Right Ideas + Right Values & Attitudes + Right Actions = Right Results – as well as the 4D Model – Define → Distill → Deliver → Drive – as shared in chapter 1.

The 4R Model is also an excellent root cause analysis tool to use when you do not obtain the Right Results. That is, you go in the opposite direction, starting from Results:

WRONG RESULTS → INCORRECT ACTIONS → INAPPROPRIATE VALUES & ATTITUDES → UNSUITABLE IDEAS

So, if you are getting the wrong results, then you need to look at the team member's actions. If the actions were incorrect, then that would be the focus of the corrective action. But, if the actions were correct, then you need to look at the Values and attitudes that were behind the actions that the person did. If the Values and attitudes were inappropriate, then this this is now the area on which to focus your corrective action. But, if the Values and Attitudes were appropriate and aligned with the Vision, then it's necessary to continue to peel back the layers of the onion even more and now look at the person's core truths or ideas. If their core truths are unsuitable for the situation or do not align with the organization, then it most likely indicates that the individual needs additional training, coaching and/or mentoring in order to get back on the right track (from a business perspective). This is also where you may have to make the determination to remove the person from the project or even the organization.

The 4R Model was Distilled from an earlier model that Andrew had learned and used during the 1980s, which is the 3R Model – Right Truth → Right Values → Right Actions. This is the model on which the 4R model is based. The 3R Model is actually the foundation and at the core of every religion, philosophy and world-life view used by anyone on the planet.

The sides of the 4R Model triangle are Mental, Physical and Social. In the 4R Model – Right Truth → Right Values & Attitudes → Right Actions → Right

Results – we originally had the individual's spirit at the center of the model and later replaced spirit with Vision (i.e. the person's Vision).

Either way, this is especially useful when working with individuals, since the 4R Model can be used to predict, within a range, how a person will behave (regardless of their core beliefs or world-view). Our observation during the past three decades is that psychologists have missed a key dimension in the genetics versus environment debate. Anyone that has held a newborn baby in their arms can immediately see and feel that the baby definitely has a hard-wired element to their personality. But, there is also the impact of the surroundings that help shape the individual (we are all victims of our environment). But, there are so many examples of people overcoming either their genetics and/or environment that we have added "choice" as the third, but most important dimension:

CHOICE (20-60%)
ENVIRONMENT (40-20%)
GENETICS (40-20%)

The 4R Model is the lens into the dimension of individual choice. Highly flexible people are much more difficult to read than someone that is inflexible— even the personality testing firms will point this out when they test individuals. People seldom like to "change" their minds, once they've made a decision. However, we have found that a key to helping individuals change their thinking and behavior is to help them make a new decision based upon new information that aligns with their Vision and the organization's Vision.

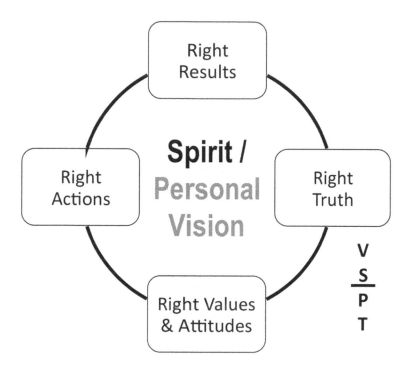

It was clear at SingTel that some of the core ideas that the individual team members had were not the "Right Ideas." For example, working 60 – 80 hours per week is not the Right Idea. It's simply not sustainable and many studies have shown that working in excess of 40 hours per week for extended periods of time is an anti-pattern that reduces productivity and quality.

Also, the Team leader had the mistaken idea that using the PMBOK, cover-to-cover, to try to Deliver the project was somehow a good idea. Anyone that has gone through our PMP exam preparation training has been taught that they should never try to use the PMBOK, cover-to-cover, to Deliver a project. It's simply a collection of good practices that the project manager can select from to Deliver their work product. No one with a deep level of project management experience would ever try to use all of the PMBOK for a single project, since they know that doing so would likely hinder them from Delivering anything of value.

As we shared in chapter 1, both of these were corrected as quickly as possible upon Andrew's arrival to Singapore. And, we trained each of the team members on the project in how to use Flow (the Unified Vision Framework) to organize and prioritize their daily work. Once the individual issues were resolved, then the individual Vision(s) could be successfully linked to the team's Vision. After the team members were trained, we experienced a very quick move of each team member into personal states of high productivity and personal Flow. This produced a team culture that began knocking out and eliminating issues, blockers and impediments that had seemed insurmountable and unsolvable just a few weeks prior.

Team transformation

"We" (Team) lens

The "We" lens is expanded upon more in chapter 2 as well as in chapters 1, 5 and 6. In these chapters we explain and expand upon how we achieved the remarkable results for the team and project at SingTel. Obviously, the team entered into a state of high-performing Flow.

Program / Product transformation

"IT" (Product / Program / PMO) lens

The original estimate for this project was in the range of $24 million. With the chaos and noise in the communication channels, Ericsson and Deloitte revised the total cost estimate to complete the project to $72 million over a five-year time frame, instead of three years as originally planned.

In reorienting the project, the original scope of the project was not altered. However, by using the "4 Whys" and 4D Model, we guided the team to understand the program and product level impacts of their actions and focused their efforts on prioritized actions that allowed them to Deliver the scope. We also saw positive impacts from the newly realized executive buy-in and aligned Visions.

Organization / Portfolio transformation

"ITS" (Organization) lens

The two key organizational change items that were essential to stopping the toxic, Flow-killing, out-of-control project noise were reducing the number of stakeholders and cutting the size of the steering group.

By focusing and aligning the team strategy from the project, team and individual perspective, the same operational team was then able to link their new Vision and strategy back to the overall Vision and strategy of SingTel. They now understood their "white hot WHY" and began to discover their path to successfully Deliver it. Organizational Flow materialized.

In addition to using the four dimensions above, Flow also utilizes the idea of small batch sizes (i.e. getting to the "one thing") as a part of improving performance.

Small Batch Sizes

"…reducing batch size is usually the single most cost-effective way to reduce queues. Smaller batches do this by reducing unnecessary variability in flow … and small batch sizes accelerate feedback." [56]

DONALD REINERTSEN

"Today's development processes typically deliver information asynchronously in large batches. A flow-based process delivers information on a regular cadence in small batches. In fact, cadence helps lower transaction costs and makes small batches more economically feasible." [57]

DONALD REINERTSEN

"…many of the most important improvements in product development, such as concurrent engineering, rapid prototyping, and agile software methods are recognizable as batch size reductions." [58]

DONALD REINERTSEN

For example, a visible product backlog is the heart and soul of Agile methodologies where work effort is broken down into Epics, Features, User Stories and Tasks. It is one of the tools used to maintain visibility for the all potential product features while controlling (as well as reducing) batch sizes in the process. This is accomplished by only taking small amounts of the total backlog to Deliver during a specific timeframe, iteration or Sprint.

In the same way, the product road map is the visual tool used for release and/or program planning. Having a decent road map is necessary for planning workflows beyond a 90-day horizon. It is never completely accurate. It is approximate, at best. The problem is that most organizations chisel the road map in stone and they become rigid in the implementation of that road map. Changes will happen along the way and a rigid, inflexible road map will block organizational Flow. Organizations that have achieved a state of Flow can quickly facilitate adapting the road map to changing conditions and new knowledge.

Like the product backlog, the product road map should be prioritized at regular and frequent intervals. The product road map's cadence should be aligned with the Flow of the individual development teams.

THE PRODUCT BACKLOG SHOULD ENCOMPASS THE ENTIRE VISION OF THE PRODUCT AND ITS DELIVERY SHOULD BE REFLECTED IN THE CONTINUOUSLY UPDATED ROAD MAP.

This requires diligent management of the product road map and a high level of discipline to decompose the product road map from the feature and epic levels down to the user story and task levels that will be used for an iteration and/or sprint.

This does not mean that the road map is a cluttered closet filled with every idea that any person or stakeholder ever suggested along the way. It needs to be honed, refined and re-prioritized against the True Vision on a regular basis. This requires a very high level of discipline and leadership.

"The world's most innovative companies are also the most disciplined. You have to have great control over the basics: only then can you start to be truly innovative." [59]

DAVID ROBERTSON

It is at the sprint level that the batch size is managed to align with the team's WIP (work in process) limits. The CEO for LEGO, Jørgen Vig Knudstorp, put the importance of narrowing focus this way:

> *"Innovation flourishes when the space available for it is limited. Less is more."* [60]

At the individual level, small batch size helps control your personal WIP (work in process) limits. WIP is the Delivery of a work item you are focused on right now. Never having more than one or two items on which you are working helps you maintain focus and increase personal productivity (your personal "one thing"). There are many studies out there that highlight and prove that multitasking reduces productivity. Reducing batch size is the organizational equivalent of eliminating the negative impacts of individual multitasking.

> *"In manufacturing, collapsing distances is one of the most powerful ways of enabling small transport batches. This is also true in product development. When we collocate development teams, we make it possible to communicate in small batches."* [61]

DONALD REINERTSEN

Less is more, small is better and proximity rules!

Move Decision Making and Governance to the Lowest Appropriate Level

"Many companies assume that the path to economic success lies in making a handful of big economic choices correctly. This leads them to concentrate decision-making authority at high levels and to design information systems that support this high-level decision-making. While big decisions are important, this bias means that most companies have weak systems to ensure that the many small economic decisions are made correctly. Collectively, these small decisions have enormous economic impact." [62] Donald Reinertsen

Jim Collins, again in "Beyond Entrepreneurship," lists a number of general principles necessary for a decentralized structure (read: Agile) to work. The very first principle is:

"Link to vision. If your vision (values, purpose, and mission) is clear, people or groups operating autonomously can self-regulate themselves relative to the shared overall vision. They can all sight on the same guiding star, yet be in separate vehicles heading toward that star. Shared vision is the crucial link in making decentralization work." [63]

To push decision-making as far down in the organization as possible requires a high level of trust in the teams from executive leadership. Collins states it well:

"This simple phrase should apply all up and down your organization: 'I trust you to do your best to do the right thing.'" [64]

Do you trust your teams?

Does your organization have a culture of trust?

Or, is it a culture of fear? If fear, then why? A culture of fear is an absolute blocker to high performance. If fear is resident in your team, begin right now to explore ways to remove it. If fear lives in the culture or leadership above you, find ways to shield your team and yourself from the toxic residue. It would be wise, right now, to take a little time to think about ways you can kill fear and build trust. You must remove fear as a blocker and/or impediment to high performance or everything else you attempt will be diminished, or fail entirely.

Fear destroys.

In "Turn the ship around" Captain Marquet describes an entire system of leader-leader management that pushes decision-making to the lowest responsible level in a culture of trust:

"… the Naval nuclear propulsion program has succeeded in developing an alternative to the personality-centered leadership approach: a procedurally-centered leadership structure in which the procedure reigns supreme. This structure is effective when it comes to operating a nuclear reactor. The system is well defined and predictable: people are highly trained and the operators follow the procedure! Actually, as a citizen of the planet, you want this procedurally centered leadership when it comes to operating the reactor plant … it is when operators don't follow procedures that very unpredictable, and typically bad, things happen … fundamentally, tactical operations

of the submarine are different from reactor plant operations. Tactical operations are against an intelligent enemy who thinks, plots, and deliberately exploits weaknesses.

"The complexity is significantly higher. Strictly following procedures won't get us there. At this point, we fall back on the personality-centered leadership structure" [65]

In the same way that VSPT and the "one thing" need to Cascade throughout the organization. Pushing power and decision making to the lowest level possible also needs to Cascade throughout the organization. For example, Captain Marquet stated:

"…Commodore Kenny was proving great leadership. He presented me with a specific goal---have Santa Fe ready for deployment in every way---but did not tell me how to do it." [66]

Having simple, clear, important and narrow objectives that are understood through the lens of Vision focuses the organization on what matters most and sets them up for achieving a higher state of Flow. Continuous prioritization against the Vision allows for quick adaptation to changing circumstances, while maintaining proper concentration on Delivering the true value.

"Merely having organizational purposes clearly defined is not a sufficient condition to experience flow, for one must also know, moment-by-moment, what precisely needs to be done and how well." [67]

By keeping the Vision and progress visible, in short cycles with small batch control, everyone in the system is aware of improvements and successes. This adds to and reinforces intrinsic motivation and helps propel transformation forward in all areas of the organization.

A Flow leader shares the Vision, but does not tell the team "how" to accomplish its Goals and thus moves decision-making and governance to the most appropriate level in the organization. Energy, high job satisfaction, high performance and an optimized state of Flow naturally ensue.

Chapter 3

Why use Flow?

"It seems that managers at all levels need a new framework and a new language to communicate with each other about projects.[68]

AARON SHENHAR AND DOV DVIR

This statement is true. And, frameworks are great. But frameworks don't implement themselves, people do. It takes leadership, skill and determination to succeed. And, ideas do have consequences:

"Knudstorp argued that for LEGO to reset its compass and authentically return to its core, 'you don't think yourself into a new way of acting, you act yourself into a new way of thinking.' 'As McKinsey consultants, we believed that thinking is paramount---that thought turns into action,' he reasoned. 'But it's actually the opposite. When you act your way into a new habit, the habit becomes your opinion about how you should do things, and that opinion becomes your character as a person or as an organization. So we started to take some actions that would make us change our behavior." [69]

DAVID ROBERTSON

Entrenched habits are hard to break. For example, overcoming fear requires repetitive, forced acts of courage. If a person is afraid of flying in an airplane, then they will not overcome that fear by not flying. Flying, the act of courage, is how you overcome the fear.

Is the person sold on the idea that flying is safe?

No.

Have they changed their minds about flying?

Absolutely not.

But, each time they step on a plane, a small yet substantial change takes place in their thinking upon the successful completion of the flight. And, that is how a new decision, based on new information, is made. Repetitive acts of courage overcome fear. And, action precedes the new way of thinking.

Knudstorp, in his old McKinsey way, actually began with an idea about how to do the change. So, in that sense, his McKinsey training was absolutely correct. However, he also understood that going through the motions, when using a new model, framework or idea, would eventually lead to an Aha! moment where both learning and transformation occur. Captain Marquet reached the same conclusion:

"Instead of trying to change mind-sets, and then change the way we acted, we would start acting differently and the new thinking would follow, or so I hoped. Besides, we didn't have time for a long gestation period. We needed change now!" [70]

In today's business environment, no one has time to wait. We all need change now! Flow and the Unified Vision Framework are the elegant simplification of all that is required to achieve the exponential results needed in today's environment. Flow is the operations manual that we use to germinate and then create high performance and fast adaptation.

It would be beautiful if you could read this book and then go back to work tomorrow and find that, magically, everything has changed. However, change requires a clear Vision and tenacious leadership. In Finnish, they call this "Sisu" or in English we would call it "perseverance." As we shared in "The Nehemiah Effect," leadership is not just a science, it is also an art. When, where and how to apply this gritty determination (i.e. Sisu) is an example of one of the intangibles that turns leadership into an art.

Leadership is required to successfully transition from initial inquiry, curiosity and hope to high-performance. We call this the "Aha! curve." This applies to individuals, teams and organizations.

Getting to Aha!

"Most companies under communicate their visions for change by at least a factor of 10."[71]

DR. JOHN KOTTER

Organizational and cultural change are difficult to achieve. Outstanding team-level results, as a launching point, does not guarantee the culture will agree or follow. Changing the entire organization usually transpires as a person-by-person and team-by-team movement toward the intended end state, until eventually the entire organization has the collective "Aha!" moment. This is, in other words, a "bottom-up" transformation requiring strong upper-level servant leadership.

This takes time and cultural anti-bodies can still rise up and crush the transformation before the desired future state for Flow is achieved. We have seen many attempts to change individual business units that were constructed and managed well, but ultimately still ended in failure. We Define "failure" as the organization returning, or snapping back, to its original state.

Transformation can also be initiated and led by senior executives. This is a top-down transition to Flow. In a healthy transformation, both bottom-up and top-down happen simultaneously.

Regardless, every level must go through the Aha! curve for Flow to occur:

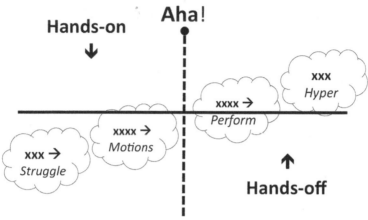

Hands-on (*Top Down*) **vs.**
Hands-off (*Bottom Up*)

We have observed that many companies mistakenly assume that adding the newest "silver bullet" process, method, framework or way of working will somehow solve their internal pain and organizational dissonance. The reality is that a new "silver bullet," be it Flow or any other new framework or method, will not save them. It still requires leadership, skill, talent, battle scars and ability to successfully implement any desired new process or change.

It really doesn't matter how well a particular "silver bullet" has worked in other organizations. Each organization is unique and therefore requires its own, customized adaptation—its own version. The Flow framework gives you the bones and elemental starting points, but a ton of work is ahead for any organization that truly desires transformative change.

As we shared in the "Intrinsic Motivation" section above, this cultural change occurs in all four areas of an organization:

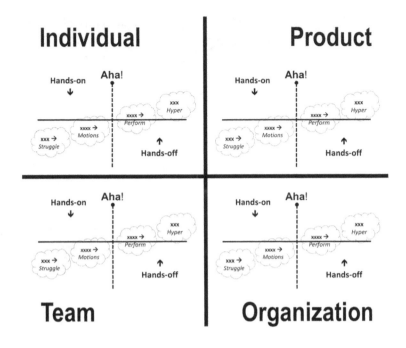

As you can see from the Flow Transformation illustrated above, you cannot change one box without impacting the other three. This is why changing the culture of an organization and achieving results using the UVF to attain Flow takes time, with or without resilient executive leadership. In fact, it takes a lot of time and discipline. Most companies are not really prepared for the amount of time needed (up to five to seven years depending upon the organization and circumstances) to make the necessary cultural changes. And, many companies do not possess the level of discipline, or grace during transition, required to achieve Flow.

There are things that can be done to accelerate the speed at which a transition happens. Skilled coaching is required.

For example, what Captain Marquet demonstrated as the senior executive and change agent during the turnaround of the Santa Fe was strong leadership combined with a culture of trust that resulted in attaining Flow in a very short time frame.

Short time frames are the exception, not the rule.

Not because the principles don't work, but because most leaders resort back to using command-and-control when situations and circumstances become uncomfortable. And, since they have found a measure of success in the past by leading this way, it becomes the default method they fall back on when things get bumpy.

However, the brilliance of what Captain Marquet Delivered was not fully described in his book, "Turn the Ship Around!" He intuitively understood the 4D and 4R Models, although he did not describe them. We will attempt to explain and help you understand the sheer genius of his approach and how he actually was using the UVF. One thing that both Marquet and Knudstorp missed, or at least was not articulated in the books describing their transformations, is that they both began with the Vision, or the Right Idea of where they wanted to end up and then acted their way to that outcome.

Captain Marquet had clear Vision of the result he wanted to obtain with his crew and was keenly aware of the restrictions created by the environment. There was no opportunity (or room) to put up visual representations of his Vision. He had to create a system to communicate and paint the picture of the cultural expectations and changes desired using only words to express his leadership style.

Historically, and according to his training, he should have jumped-in and demanded changes according to what he knew were best practices. Instead, and in large part because he no training in the Santa Fe class submarine he was now commanding, he pushed authority down to the lowest level in the organization and allowed the teams to come up with the best way to accomplish the work themselves. He explains the Navy approach as follows:

"Here's what my Naval Academy leadership book told me about being a leader: 'Leadership is the art, science or gift by which a person is enabled and privileged to direct the thoughts, plans, and actions of others in such a manner as to obtain and command their obedience, their confidence, their respect, and their loyal cooperation.' In other words, leadership in the Navy, and in most organizations, is about controlling people ... people can accomplish a tremendous amount through the leader-follower model, particularly with adept bosses ... many bosses and owners got rich, and the followers were better off too. It is exactly because the leader-follower way of doing business has been so successful that it is both so appealing and so hard to give up."[72]

Captain Marquet implemented a leader-leader, or servant-leader, model instead. This is a core principle of the UVF and Flow. He started with clear Definitions, but in a flash of insight he focused on the actions required for changes that were needed (as cited in the beginning of this chapter). In other words, he went from **Definitions (D1)** to **Right Actions (R3)** and moved backwards through the 4R Model from that point and attained exponential results (Right Actions → Right Values & Attitudes → Right Ideas → Right Results). For a more thorough explanation of the 4R Model, see Chapter 2.

What is amazing is that he didn't need to align the individual's ideas with his ideas. Since they could comprehend the actions required, they were able to implement the Vision. The success and positive impacts of the actions led to the ultimate change in thinking (i.e. it was caused by Defining actions and doing them).

David Allen in his book, "Getting Things Done" agrees with Captain Marquet:

"What you do with your time, what you do with information, and what you do with your body and your focus relative to your priorities---those are the real options to which you must allocate your limited resources. The real issue is how to make appropriate choices about what to 'do' at any point in time. The real issue is how we manage actions."[73]

Andrew observed this same effect at Nature Publishing Group when, two years into an Agile transformation, a couple of board members remarked to the CTO that they were amazed at how the words used to communicate in an Agile, or Flow way had so dramatically changed the communications at the Board and executive levels. Using the principles of the UVF, he achieved a similar, powerful result, like Captain Marquet did, with the Santa Fe.

Results

Every organization wants positive and profitable results as Defined by their Vision. Non-profits and NGOs want to accomplish their service Mission. Governments want to maintain social order and healthy environments. Businesses want to grow profitably and be an asset to society.

However, without a profit or a net-positive revenue stream, whatever you are doing is not sustainable. And, unless the team is self-funded, it reports to someone and is accountable to him or her for the results they produce, regardless of organizational type or context.

Freeing teams to be creative and innovative in a healthy, high-performance environment makes business sense, human sense and is ultimately common sense. This, along with the proper constraints, leadership and governance enable the achievement of economically and socially sustainable results.

And, in the best cases, they facilitate and Deliver it.

It is not "either-or," it is "both-and."

If you desire to move into a both-and environment as we describe above, but your personal actions do not line up with your words, then your teams will find it hard to align, focus and Deliver. They will be confused and this risks disempowering them. Again, Marquet says it well:

"You can't 'direct' empowerment programs. Directed empowerment programs are flawed because they are predicated on this assumption: I have the authority and ability to empower you (and you don't). Fundamentally, that's disempowering. This internal contradiction dooms these initiatives. We say 'empowerment' but do it in a way that is disempowering. The practice outweighs the rhetoric." [74]

So, anything that disempowers your teams will block Delivery of your desired results. Flow consistently Delivers results—results aligned with Vision.

Chapter 4

Who is involved in transforming to Flow?

Everyone in the organization should be involved, from the Board of Directors and CEO on down. Yes, we know that this sounds very hierarchical, but our experience is that this is the case. Having a hierarchical structure is not inherently evil. Captain Marquet demonstrated this in his book "Turn the Ship Around," which we have quoted often.

Executive team buy-in is essential to any organizational transformation. One of the toughest parts of any change effort is obtaining the full backing and participation of the Board of Directors and executives. Recognizing the need for change requires that they have the unusual ability to look in the mirror and confront the brutal fact that they themselves actually need to change first. There is an old Greek proverb that states: "the fish rots from the head." It takes a remarkably self-assured and humble executive to be able to accept that change is needed at his or her level. Doing so allows the organization itself to determine how the desired change should be implemented in a self-directed and self-governed way.

If the Board or executives are unable or unwilling to go through the required personal transformation, then there is not much that can be done to affect change across the entire organization. The best that can be hoped for is change at the level from which you lead. However, you must realize that this counter-cultural approach is dangerous and difficult. As we stated above, cultural anti-bodies rise up and kill any foreign body (i.e. ideas for change or improvement) that attempts to enter the system.

There are a few issues with teams that team-level Agile methodologies tend to sweep under the rug and avoid.

First, group communications theory and dynamics teach that in any group leaders naturally emerge. Most Agile methodologies, in practice, attempt to override this. Scrum, for example, attempts to put in a constraint to mitigate this natural part of team formation. It declares that the team is the "leader." They believe that consensus leadership by the team is more powerful than having an individual team leader. Thus, any leader naturally emerging from within a team is prevented from doing what comes naturally to them: leading. This is actually a form of inverted command-and-control. Also, not allowing organic leadership to rise up and be recognized is an anti-pattern that constricts and prevents Flow. It also diminishes the need for all organizations to create a leadership "pool" that recognizes and develops future leaders.

While we agree that a high-performing team has strong input from all team members, you cannot ignore the natural dynamic of leadership.

Agile methodologies many times state that servant leadership is best. We agree. But, without mentoring and coaching, can we rely on servant leaders to naturally emerge in each and every team 100% of the time? Or can the team itself behave like a servant leader? Our experience is that servant leadership is the exception, not the rule and that for leadership growth, coaching and mentoring is required.

Second, the other issue we have found is a reluctance (bordering on violent opposition) to recognizing the role and importance of superstars.

One of the "poster child" examples of an effective, fully Agile organization that leverages organic leadership growth and recognizes superstar performance is Menlo Innovations in Ann Arbor, Michigan, USA. Menlo has C-level leadership and mid-level project managers in addition to high-performing Agile teams. They would not be Defined as "fully Agile" by many Agile coaches. However, they are massively productive, successful and profitable.

They are an interesting example of how to achieve both leadership and growth while maintaining a healthy, strong team dynamic. Rich Sheridan, the founder and CEO, was the keynote at the Scrum Gathering in the US during 2014. He got a standing ovation at the end of his presentation. Ted visited their office and observed a wall where all seven Menlo pay grades were shown and also which employees were at which level. James Goebel, co-founder and Chief Innovation Officer, was showing Ted around and explained that the only way that someone moves up in pay grade was by a vote of the entire organization. In other words, they recognize organic growth and leadership in a visible and tangible way.

How simple.

How profound.

How excellent and cool.

Menlo's approach is one way to ensure that team results don't obscure individual performance. It needs to be recognized that stars will naturally emerge on any team. Both the teams and the stars on each team need to be recognized and compensated for the additional value that they bring.

While this may run counter to normal Agile ideals, it addresses reality.

People will leave if they believe they are not being treated fairly or if the process for compensation is not transparent. When Michael Jordan was leading the Chicago Bulls to consistent playoff victories, who would want to suggest his raking in a lion's share of the compensation was somehow unfair? What many people may not know is that Michael actually took a smaller salary so that they could bring in better talent on the team and still stay under the mandated salary cap for the NBA. An act of servant-leadership on Michael's part ensured that they could build a cohesive, unified, high-performing championship team. Michael's genius in taking less salary was that it created more wealth (long-term) for him, the Bulls and his teammates.

He is still enjoying the fruit of those decisions.

The same idea applies to teams in organizations as well. In fact, in his presentation at the Agile Gathering West Michigan in September of 2015, Dr.

David Rico shared that only "1 developer in a 1,000 is a superstar." Most Agile environments do not recognize, reward or facilitate superstar performance. The focus and compensation is only on the team level, not the individual level. We believe this is a flaw in Agile environments that needs to be addressed and corrected.

Third, many Agilists tend to bristle at the concept of "command-and-control" at the team level. What they miss is that a key "command-and-control" constraint that is employed by many Agile methodologies is the role of Product Owner. Why is that? Because the Product Owner is the single, wringable neck and he or she has the final say if the incremental product, service or result produced by the team during a sprint (time-boxed iteration) will be accepted. They absolutely control the end result and product Delivered by the team (read "command-and-control"). Here again the underlying assumption is that the Product Owner is competent, has full authority and operates as a servant leader. This single point of failure is one of the main reasons we have found for some Agile projects not succeeding.

So, in that sense, Agile, Scrum and other methods are at war with themselves on this issue. You risk ending up with too many chefs in the kitchen (i.e. the team vs. Product Owner vs. upper management, etc.).

Is the Product Owner the true leader of the team?

Or, does the team lead itself?

Of course, no one is allowed to tell the team "how" to get its work done. But, since the Product Owner owns, prioritizes and reprioritizes the Product Backlog, they have the final say on what work is ultimately done by the team.

Collaboration and agreement must occur between the Product Owner and the team. The team works on the highest prioritized backlog work items as Defined by the Product Owner. The team does not decide that prioritization. They only decide on "how" the work will be done once they accept the work that has been agreed to for the next iteration or Sprint.

The last group of stakeholders that need to be on board for a transformation is middle management. Agile purists see no value-add in having extra layers of middle management. They would prefer to eliminate those levels completely.

In trying to go "Agile," removing middle management roles across-the-board may end up being a very expensive mistake for many organizations.

It may even prove to be fatal.

Organizations should be very careful when eliminating roles that have valuable organizational knowledge. It may require redefinition and repurposing. When doing a transformation, it would be wise to err to the side of caution and fully investigate the true value-add of the roles before eliminating them.

Transitioning to Flow should be an organization-wide exercise. Whenever possible, everyone should be included and involved. Some of the most outstanding value-adds created by Flow have been in situations where everyone was part of the transformation. DNA Finland, and the results achieved there, is a really good example (see case study in Appendix A).

MUST HAVES FOR CREATING, ENTERING AND MAINTAINING FLOW

Chapter 5

The Flow Formula for Success

We have Distilled Flow into a formula for creating successful organizations:

Vision + Right People + the 4D Model = Success

For the case studies included in Appendix A (and also shared in part in these chapters), we use the Flow formula above along with the four lenses on transformation – **I, We, It and Its** – at the project and organizational levels, to demonstrate Flow. In the following section, we apply this format to the SingTel case study, starting with Vision.

Vision

"If you are working on something exciting that you really care about, you don't have to be pushed. The vision pulls you." [75]

STEVE JOBS

"The most pathetic person in the world is someone who has sight but has no vision." [76]

HELEN KELLER

Yes, and if you are not led, pushed and pulled by Vision, then you will be driven a thousand different directions (all at once), by circumstances. If your circumstances are driving you, don't give up. There is hope and help is on the way.

If you are involved in working with people, processes, projects, programs, products, services or results, then you are automatically working with change (individual, team, product and organizational).

> *"The most common sign of absent vision (is) the sense of not knowing 'who we are.'"* [77]
>
> **TOM DEMARCO**

In order to help SingTel, understand who they were and to create the right environment for project success, we clarified the SingTel project's Vision and linked it to the overall Vision of the organization. As we shared in Chapter 1, the Project Vision was Distilled into a short, easy-to-communicate Vision statement of *"enabling the successful launch of the Pod Brand."*

We read a statistic recently from Donald Reinertsen that *"96% of new products fail to meet their economic objectives."* [78] What is stunning about this statistic is that the high level of product development failure is even worse than project or change management failure rates (roughly 70% of all change efforts and up to 58% of project management efforts fail). This failure rate applies to all project management methodologies and scaled frameworks, regardless of whether they use Traditional/Waterfall, Lean/Kanban or Agile/Scrum, etc. There is an old proverb that says:

"Where there is no vision, the people perish." [79]

Another translation of the same proverb puts it this way:

"Where there is no vision, the people cast off restraint." [80]

Casting off restraint conveys the idea of letting all of the horses out of the barn and then watching them run off in all directions at once as they disappear over the horizon. Every team member ends up doing what is right in his or her own eyes, regardless of whether or not it achieves the Vision.

In our experience a failure to clearly Define and articulate Vision is one of the primary reasons for the abysmal failure rates of all the situations shared above. Hopefully your efforts to turn things around or implement a successful cultural change will be part of the 30% of change programs that succeed. Being able to do a successful organizational change is a rare commodity in the business world. There are entire groups and teams that are solely dedicated to guiding organizations through the turbulence that change naturally creates. If you are leading this type of effort, please make sure your Vision is clear and communicated well.

We also include the "4 Whys" as part of Vision since there are only 4 Purposes for doing anything in a company. In "The Nehemiah Effect" we had quoted Paul DiModica and shared his "3 Why" rationale for developing a value-proposition:

"Management buying decisions are centered around three elements:

1. How to increase income
2. How to decrease expenses
3. How to manage their business risks." [81]

We like Paul's structure and agree with its simplicity, but modified it since "The Nehemiah Effect" into the following 4 Purposes as the reasoning for doing a project, product or service as follows:

1. Increase revenues,
2. Decrease costs; and,
3. Get rid of or mitigate risks; and,
4. Doing the right thing.

Done correctly, these four items identify the metrics that can be used to obtain a clean Definition of "done." Vision is still the key. It is your most important starting point in the journey to Flow. And, of course, it takes the Right People to get anything of value done and Deliver the Vision.

Right People

Additionally, we needed to make sure that the SingTel project had the Right People on the team. This was especially true since Ericsson and Deloitte were ready to fire everyone and start over, assuming that the problem resided with the project team. However, upon further investigation, we found that it wasn't the team that was the issue. Rather, it was the management processes that were broken just like Deming told Henry Ford:

> "To Ford's surprise, Deming talked not about quality but about management. He told Ford that management actions were responsible for 85% of all problems in developing better cars." [82]

So, after a quick assessment, we determined that the project had the Right People onboard.

And, by bringing clarity to the Definitions related to stakeholders, steering committee, complexity of the project plan and reporting, we were able to Distill agreement with SingTel's executives. Once this was complete, we re-planned and reoriented the existing project team to Deliver and drive success based on the fresh understanding and agreements. Once a Flow structure (including self-organization and self-governance) was in place and agreed to, the team was able to quickly move into a state of high performance.

Define
Putting the Right Definitions (D1) into the plan, including "Done"

At SingTel, the original 440 stakeholders had succeeded in creating a very high level of confusion by putting over 2,000 lines of work items into the project plan and trying to manage all of those lines every week. This created a level of noise that a team of eight or nine people simply could not manage. There is no way any team could manage the flow of Definitions, requirements, specifications, etc., pouring in from 96,580 communication channels created by having 440 stakeholders ($440 * 439 / 2 = 96,580$) actively involved. A 91% reduction in Stakeholders resulted in a 99% reduction in communication channel noise.

It's no surprise that the team was confused and paralyzed.

Reducing the number of communication channels is always a great place to start when the situation is confusing because aligning 440 stakeholders and 38 steering committee members is virtually an impossible task. Even worse, getting a mob that size to agree on Definitions was unmanageable and unwieldy.

So, one of the first clear Definitions that we established was to reduce the number of stakeholders. Establishing an agreement that only 38 of the 440 stakeholders needed to be actively involved. This was not easy to implement, but it was absolutely necessary. The remaining stakeholders not actively involved were kept in the loop and updated via a monthly newsletter.

The steering committee was also reduced from 38 down to 12. Using the communications formula, shared above, this reduced the 703 potential communication channels down to only 66 (12 * 11 / 2 = 66). Reducing the number of Steering Committee members by 69% resulted in a 91% reduction in the total number of potential communication channels for the team.

Once the downsized Steering Committee was put in place, we did an exercise where we put the 40 weekly reports up on the wall and had them put a check mark on the ones that they had read at least one time during the previous six months.

Only four reports got at least one check.

Those were the four reports we issued over the next 30 days. This eliminated 36 reports (a 90% reduction) plus all of the effort to create them. After 30 days, the Steering Committee determined that only 2 reports were actually useful and those were the reports we continued to issue for the balance of the project.

The team Defined the top 200 items in the project plan that could be Delivered in next 90 days resulting in our new Definition of "done." The Steering Committee was tasked with reviewing and approving the new plan, which they did, thus "parking" over 1,800 lines of work items from the old plan (which, by the way, were never needed or completed).

Distill
Distilling Agreement (D2) between the warring tribes

"In a pure consensus style, the group makes the decision. The leader does not impose her solution, but rather seeks a choice that has 'general agreement' among the entire group. The leader's skill is in asking questions, making observations, providing input, and catalyzing a decision. Effective consensus leaders guide the group to closure at just the right time---they don't cut off

the process prematurely, nor do they let deliberations drag on unproductively. Consensus does not equal unanimity!" [83]

JIM COLLINS AND WILLIAM LAZIER

"In general, the most effective leaders tend to make extensive use of participative decision making. The best decisions are made with some degree of participation---no one is brilliant or experienced enough to have all of the answers. No one." [84]

JIM COLLINS AND WILLIAM LAZIER

When a "mob" has taken over and is running the show, not only do you have an incredible level of politics, but also incorrect assumptions about what is happening and must happen for the project to succeed. This leads to a continuous flood of problems, including 4-hour stakeholder meetings where nothing is accomplished, except identifying more problems and blaming others for failure.

An inability to understand and grasp how quickly politics can kill a project, product, service or result is one of the major causes of project failure in both Agile and Traditional situations. "Purists" in the Agile movement have done themselves no favors by declaring "management" as the source of all evil in the world. We have actually witnessed an Agile Coach voicing that opinion multiple times to both customers and co-workers.

The result was toxic and unfortunate.

Politics and a toxic project environment were overwhelming the SingTel team as well. But, by reducing the number stakeholders and the size of the steering committee, the political noise was greatly reduced, almost to zero. Also, since items that did not align with the Vision **were** eliminated from the agenda of the weekly status meeting, we were able to reduce the time box for that meeting from four hours to one hour in duration. Remember Parkinson's Law:

"Work expands so as to fill the time available for its completion." [85]

WIKIPEDIA

The steering committee and project team Distilled agreement on the new agenda based upon the re-prioritized and simplified work effort. Simple, effective and the noise and politics abated.

That's the power of agreement.

The power of Flow.

The team began to experience a successful Delivery.

Deliver
Delivering (D3) the Project began to Flow

> *"'Vision without execution is just hallucination' is actually the favorite saying of serial entrepreneur, Steve Adams (and) is a variation on an ancient Japanese proverb, 'Vision without action is a daydream.'"* [86]
>
> **BRYAN STOLLE**

Simplifying the project plan at SingTel was "interesting."

Simplifying, particularly in a situation that's on fire, is seldom a calm exercise. For example, it was not stress-free to gain agreement from all of the stakeholders that we would cut over 1,800 lines of work or reduce the number of reports from 40 down to 2. It almost resulted in a literal riot.

It's puzzling to us that any organization would not immediately recognize the return on the investment available through simplification and start on the journey of simplifying everything they do at every level in the enterprise. However, many times the negative inertia of the existing corporate culture keeps things the way they are, regardless of how broken or misdirected.

It is not enough to recognize that simplicity is needed.

It is required and strong action is needed.

One of the principles (number 10 of 12) behind the Agile Manifesto is:

"Simplicity---the art of maximizing the amount of work not done---is essential." [87]

Issuing 40 reports where only 2 were needed is one small example of the power of this principle. To our way of thinking, the principle of simplicity is the most important of all 12 principles.

Using Flow and the Unified Vision Framework, Andrew successfully simplified, maximizing the amount of work not done on the project at SingTel. One of the key principles of lean is to find "Muda," or waste, and eliminate it. Using a simple framework to sort and structure the tasks necessary for success eliminated enormous amounts of unnecessary work, waste and effort for the team.

Every organization, portfolio, program, and project, etc., has pivot points.

The trick is to identify those and then manage them without disturbing the organization's existing culture, unless cultural change is required. A seasoned leader should be able to quickly recognize the pivot points (patterns and anti-patterns) and act accordingly to Deliver the corrective action(s) needed to turn the situation around.

By the way, simplifying above the team level at the Program and Portfolio levels gets even more complex. We have seen that Ron Jefferies, one of the signers of the Agile Manifesto, has often been quoted in discussion threads and at conferences as having said "don't try to scale Agile." We're not able to validate the accuracy of that quote, but have heard and read it, second hand, on numerous occasions. We agree that team Agile does not scale. Vision scales.

There are a limited number of Agilists that have actually successfully scaled Agile to an entire organization, however they did it using Vision. The skill and experience to be able to do this is quite unique.

We do not believe it is enough to take a successful team-level Agile coach and promote them to an Enterprise Agile coach role. Unless an Agile coach has set-up and run an Agile portfolio or, at minimum, an Agile program management Office (PMO), then they probably don't have enough skill, experience or wisdom to know what land mines to avoid. One of the keys to creating a successful Agile PMO is knowing which tools to throw out; and, more importantly, which to keep and/or adapt to Agile.

Recently, on the Agile Sweden mail list there was a rather long discussion thread asking for examples of "traditional" Swedish companies that have actually successfully transitioned from Waterfall to Agile. The members of the forum were hard-pressed to come up with even a single, successful example. If there are no examples of successful Swedish transformations, then that might indicate that there is a huge market out there of companies that need training, coaching and mentoring.

This is one of the reasons that we decided to share so many case studies in this book. Flow can enable your successful transformation regardless of the team-level methodologies or frameworks that are used by the enterprise. Flow takes the organization beyond Traditional, Lean and Agile. Flow creates a laser focus by Distilling agreement on the Definitions for your product, project, process, service or result, and it Delivers and drives that in all four lenses of the "I, We, It and Its" windows of transformation, just like it did on the SingTel project.

Drive
Driving (D4) to Success!

> *"Applying the adaptive approach to a project need not be difficult. First, you treat project execution as an iterative, not a linear, process. This means that you may need to go back to project definition and project planning based on the project's initial uncertainties and later findings during execution."* [88]
> **AARON SHENHAR AND DOV DVIR**

By eliminating the division that had taken root in the SingTel project, team, stakeholders and sponsors, we were able to quickly turn the situation from in flames and out-of-control to a high-performing, exceptional Delivery.

The results speak for themselves:

- ☐ The project completed seven months early instead of two years late (five months after we were engaged to assist).
- ☐ There was an actual savings of $4 million, instead of the potential increased costs of $48 million.

Every webinar, conference audience or group that we have shared this example with has had the same reaction to the results:

Wow!

Can you come help us do the same thing?

The answer is yes.

However, you don't need us to accomplish Flow.

Utilize the Flow framework and the power of Vision and simplicity. Use short time-frames and small batches and you will achieve better results.

As we shared in the SingTel case study, no one, not even the executives at Ericsson or Deloitte, believed that the project could be saved. The SingTel executives were very unhappy and ready to pull the plug on the project as well.

Earlier, we asked you to put yourself in Andrew's shoes.

You have just been sent from Stockholm, Sweden to Singapore to not just "rescue" this project disaster; but, to turn it around and Deliver it on time, on budget and on-scope within a 90-day time-frame. We shared, from the team level perspective, how we successfully did this.

Being able to manage and Deliver each of the 4-boxes for transformation effectively is what Flow is all about and is a perfect example of the Nehemiah Effect described in our first book where people step-back, are stunned by the results, and all they can say is, "Wow! How did that happen?!"

As we stated in the beginning of this chapter, the formula we use to attain a state of Flow is simple:

Vision + Right People + the 4D Model = Success

We are extremely aware that simple is not easy.

So, along with Andrew and Ted, there is a growing group of Flow Certified Professionals and Trainers that are available to train, coach and mentor your organization using the formula above to achieve Flow, a sustainable state of high-performance.

SECTION 3:
ANTI-FLOW

Chapter 6

Antipatterns that Block Flow

"Are you and your people working to optimize the organization for their tenure, or forever? To promote long-term success, I had to ignore the short-term reward system" [89]

DAVID MARQUET

"Focusing on avoiding mistakes takes our focus away from being truly exceptional." [90]

DAVID MARQUET

The team at SingTel was experiencing "anti-Flow" (organizational constipation) when Andrew arrived. And, if you look at the Vision Flow formula we share below, they were experiencing every anti-flow result possible: anxiety, confusion, politics, chaos and caustic division. Is it any wonder this project was not Delivering the desired results and was totally out of control? So, we used Flow in its earliest iterations to do the corrective actions needed to turn this project around.

To be successful your organization requires a proper Vision Flow.

If you don't have Vision Flow and you are experiencing challenges, use the chart below to quickly identify the root cause(s), so that you can take corrective action.

Flow = Vision + Right People + 4D Model
*4D Model = Define (**D1**) → Distill (**D2**) →*
*Deliver (**D3**) → Drive (**D4**)*

$$■ + RP + D1 + D2 + D3 + D4 = \text{Anarchy}$$

$$\text{Vision} + ■ + D1 + D2 + D3 + D4 = \text{Anxiety}$$

$$\text{Vision} + RP + ■ + D2 + D3 + D4 = \text{Confusion}$$

$$\text{Vision} + RP + D1 + ■ + D3 + D4 = \text{Politics}$$

$$\text{Vision} + RP + D1 + D2 + ■ + D4 = \text{Chaos}$$

$$\text{Vision} + RP + D1 + D2 + D3 + ■ = \text{Division}$$

This is the latest version of the chart we used to turn the SingTel project around in less than 90 days. Simplification achieved by using the above diagram to do a high-speed gap analysis is both art and science.

This demands going beyond merely doing a few business process reengineering exercises or workshops and then calling it "good enough."

Fractured Organizational Vision results in Anarchy

A Vision that is unclear, poorly communicated or completely missing is the number one anti-pattern blocking Flow. A clear indicator that Vision is absent or unclear is the presence of anarchy. If you are experiencing anarchy, then look to problems with Vision as a potential root cause.

An operational subset of this anti-pattern is assuming that the wisdom of the crowd trumps visionary leadership. It hopes that a clear Vision will somehow organically emerge from the bottom-up. However, even if an over-arching Vision were to emerge successfully from the team level, there is no way to know if it would arrive in time to mitigate or eliminate anarchy in the organization or have a positive outcome.

For example, at LEGO the situation back in 2003 was dire:

"The family fortune had been depleted at a rate of almost half a million dollars per day, for the previous ten years … the immediate future looked even bleaker than its recent past. The company was on track to suffer a 30% drop in sales and bleed out $250 million in operating costs. It was running a negative cash flow of more than $160 million. By year's end LEGO would likely default on its outstanding debt of nearly $800 million, and it lacked committed lines of credit. The forecast for 2004 looked every bit as ugly, if not worse, as the company's net loss was expected to double … 94% of LEGO sets were unprofitable. Only Star Wars and Bionicle kits were making money. Not only had LEGO sustained the largest losses, on a percentage basis, among toy makers, it was by far the industry's least profitable brand." [91]

DAVID ROBERTSON

It is highly unlikely that a holacracy, through an organic, bottom-up creation of Vision, would have had sufficient time to experiment its way forward to a proper, True Vision before being engulfed in the flames of anarchy.

The crowd could not make the leadership call.

The business press and many leaders in Lego's organization thought that Lego was "DOA" (dead on arrival). However, leadership and organizational restructuring utilizing the elements that we describe here in Flow, completely turned the LEGO ship around:

"While Mattel's and Hasbro's sales between 2007 and 2011 grew at an annual rate of 1 percent and 3 percent, respectively, the LEGO Group's sales surged at a rate of 24% per year. In 2012, LEGO reported a 27 percent increase in sales and a 36 percent increase in profits over the previous year, for a 5-year average annual sales growth of 24 percent and annual profit growth of 40 percent." [92]

DAVID ROBERTSON

This was not done using a holacracy.

This was achieved through leadership at the executive level and through freedom, within constraints, at the team level. You can have a strong hope or desire that holacracy will create a healthy governance environment. However, the reality is that group-based leadership does not set constraints. Leadership sets the limits and hopefully, in wisdom, frees teams and individuals to innovate within clear boundaries.

We have yet to witness any viable example where holacracy has generated the True Vision of an organization from the bottom-up. On the other hand, there are many examples, like LEGO, where the organization thrived and flourished because the leadership narrowed its Vision and utilized the elements described here in Flow. Again, Robertson emphasizes:

"LEGO is an inspired innovator, but it doesn't operate out on the fringes of business experience. There is no 20% time at LEGO and there are plenty of titles. Having seen how some of the business world's most popular strategies for unleashing innovation almost destroyed their company, the LEGO Group's leaders instead built a clear framework for guiding every kind of innovation effort, from improving today's offerings to inventing tomorrow's markets." [93]

Many Agile practitioners believe that all hierarchy is bad, borders on evil and therefore should be eliminated. If only it were that simple. All organizations, as they grow, should assess each and every function, team and/or department that exists or that they plan to put into place and determine whether or not there is a value Delivered by its existence or creation. It's not a question of hierarchy; it is a question of value. And a holacratic, time consuming, organic, bottom-up decision-making governance approach, will not extinguish a blazing inferno of anarchy or cure an environment that lacks trust.

Leadership and organization matters and not all organizational hierarchy is evil. This is one idea, in our opinion, that needs to be eliminated from Agile thinking and cultures.

If we look at this from an anthropological perspective, humans are hard-wired, in a group setting, for leaders to naturally emerge. Nigel Nicholson stated this eloquently in a Harvard Business Review article:

"The Dilbert characters seem to know what any evolutionary psychologist would tell you: hierarchy is forever. The truth is that leaders are born, not made. They are not clones, but all of them share one special personality trait: a passion to lead." [94]

Since leaders arise during the normal course of human group dynamics, then why place an unnatural constraint (like holacracy) on the organically emerging leader? This limits the performance of the group to the lowest common denominator.

Moreover, this dilutes Vision and is an anti-pattern to high-performance.

Although group-based decision-making seldom limits innovation, good leadership sets limits and priorities, even within Agile and Scrum environments. This frees teams and individuals to fully innovate within the Defined and agreed-upon constraints. As we mentioned earlier, unrestricted creativity and innovation almost destroyed LEGO. They acted to implement constraints and simplified and organized around the latest iteration of the Vision of LEGO which is *"to inspire and develop the builders of tomorrow."* [95] They forced themselves to innovate inside the box. As Knudstorp stated, *"innovation flourishes when the space available for it is limited. Less is more."* [96]

Not communicating your passion for your Vision often (ten times more than what we think we need to do) may lead to anti-flow that could choke your team's creativity. It also risks creating "innovation" that adds no value to your organization. Creativity does not spring up from nothing. It has a foundation, structure and constraints within which it lives.

That foundation for an organization is its Vision.

The culture created by that Vision is the environment that will either enable creativity to thrive or potentially block the organization's possibilities for valuable innovation.

We have also observed that a culture of fear creates an anti-Flow environment. This is another way that a fractured organizational Vision manifests itself because fear stops Flow at the individual, team and ultimately organizational levels.

For those of you that read our first book, "The Nehemiah Effect," you will remember that we include Mission, Purpose, core Values and attitudes along with Goals and Objectives as part of Vision and culture. In order for Cascading Vision and the "one thing" to function properly in any organization you have to have the Right People and culture backing it up. If that culture is based on fear, you will never reach a state of high-performing Flow.

Fear as a motivator only works in short bursts of time to accomplish a specific Purpose. Leaving your teams in a constant "fight or flight" mode as cultural norm will burn them out. If you use fear too long, it is an anti-flow pattern that needs to be corrected and eliminated from the organization. Eventually the teams grow immune to the tool and ignore the fear while under-performing.

The Lego example above had elements of short-term fear that were utilized in the early stages of the turnaround. The real fear was, that unless things changed, Lego would cease to exist as an organization. This helped clarify the steps needed to correct the situation. The fear of death always brings clarity. Once the corrections were made, fear was no longer a part of the management approach or culture.

Leadership will always be required to identify and eliminate fractured organizational Vision, regardless of how it manifests itself.

Anxiety due to Wrong People

Anxiety can spring from many sources. But, along with Vision, VSPT and the "one thing," having the Right People is vital to your success. However, having the wrong people involved in the project nearly guarantees an anxious undercurrent for the team.

Anxiety rises because confidence in eventual success is reduced.

If you are not confident that your teammates or co-workers can pull off the job, it will increase your anxiety. Also, if you do not think that you personally have the skills, talents and abilities necessary to get the job done, your anxiety and the anxiety of your teammates will increase.

Having the wrong people, in any functional area can weaken, or even completely destroy, Flow. However, the most important "Right People" person needs to be the leader. This is true at the team level and every other level in an organizational structure. For example, Menlo Innovations would not be in existence today apart from the Vision and leadership of Richard Sheridan. The Santa Fe went from worst to best of class and then to best in the history of Naval operations via the Vision and leadership of David Marquet. Same crew, different results. Lego transformed itself from a bankrupt organization on the fast track to oblivion to a stunningly productive and profitable company when the children of the founders had the wisdom and humility to bring in (and listen to, we might add) Jørgen Knudstorp. His leadership refocused the organization on the True Vision of Lego. The Agile principles that he successfully applied operationally might never have succeeded without his leadership and focus on Vision. In a similar vein, Andrew's success at SingTel required leadership, as did the other case studies at the end of this book.

The right solution to combat anxiety is to identify, authorize and release the Right People leader.

Frankly, the most important task at the executive level is to cultivate and grow leaders. At the highest level, it is to also create a leadership growth culture (where all leaders are servant leaders) throughout the entire organization.

Choosing a poor or toxic leader can result in an organizational cancer, which ultimately kills-off the body of its host. If coaching, education and direction don't bring alignment, it is probably time to cut the cancer out and to start fresh. As Zig Ziglar paraphrased it, you need to:

"Eliminate the pool of poison since no company is big enough to have that much toxin concentrated in a single person and survive," [97]

Speaking of toxic poison that needs to be dealt with or removed, the most downloaded and reprinted article in the history of the Harvard Business Review is *"The No Asshole Rule"* [98] by Stanford Business Professor Robert Sutton. His subsequent book by the same name was a New York Times best seller and has had a profound impact on organizations around the world. His book can be simply summed up as *'everybody has one, but no one should have to work with one.'*

We agree with Mr. Ziglar and Mr. Sutton that toxic people kill great ideas, teams or organizations. Do everything within your power to protect yourself, your team or organization from these people. Mr. Sutton gives us two rules worth utilizing in identifying these toxins:

"Test One: After talking to the alleged asshole, does the "target" feel oppressed, humiliated, de-energized, or belittled by the person? In particular, does the target feel worse about him or herself? [99]

Test Two: Does the alleged asshole aim his or her venom at people who are less powerful rather than at those people who are more powerful?" [100]

Once a toxic person has been identified, plans need to be made and executed to mitigate the harmful effects; and, if possible, remove the source.

If you want to have a little fun, we came across an App where you can measure yourself against your friends, family or well-known public assholes. It has a clever URL that even our Baptist, Sunday-school teaching mother would have approved: www.appholeindex.com. If you would like to know how we ranked, send us an email, but you will have to disclose your ranking as well.

Assholes at any level of the organization are harmful. It is magnified in Agile environments, especially regarding the Product Owner role. The role of Product Owner is critical for Scrum or Agile teams to succeed. Having a Product Owner who is an asshole can absolutely kill Flow.

By the way, having the Certified Scrum Product Owner (CSPO) is not necessarily an indication of competence, skill or ability.

The last time we checked, there were around 50,000 CSPOs in the Scrum Alliance and there are over 450,000 Certified Scrum Masters. The disparity in this ratio between CSPOs and CSMs is a major disconnect for the successful Delivery of Agile or Scrum projects. The Product Owner owns the product backlog and has the final say (i.e. command-and-control) of the acceptance or rejection of the results of the sprint or release. With too few CSPOs available to work with Scrum teams, the fall back is to create Proxy Product Owners. This diminishes the positive impact a strong, well performing Product Owner brings to the team.

We have gotten feedback from people that have gone through CSPO training that observed that they learned little to nothing about true Product Ownership. Depending on the trainer, up to 75 percent of the CSPO training is nothing more than a repeat of the CSM training. So, even having a Product Owner with a CSPO certification is no guarantee that person will be competent to understand and lead the Product Ownership role. A weak or incompetent Product Owner (or proxy Product Owner) will almost always guarantee a poor result for your project. Conversely:

"Product owners have to have sufficient authority to make decisions by themselves, have enough vision to define the product, and have enough leadership to deliver results. Ideally, they're good at everything. They need to have enough management skills to know what they can do themselves and what they need to delegate. They need leadership, vision, and a deep knowledge of the product, combined with the ability to prioritize and make decisions. Such people are very rare and need to be developed. Product owners like that are able to make good product backlogs. Giving a well-oiled Scrum team a good backlog can make the impossible happen." [101]

JEFF SUTHERLAND

The Product Owner is just one role, but obviously a very important role. And, if you are in an Agile environment, however you decide to build your team, you will still need to make sure that you have the Right People involved. It only takes one person with a bad or toxic attitude to negatively affect everyone else on the team. This is particularly true when the toxic person is the Product Owner. Having the wrong people on a project in any role can create unnecessary noise and heartburn. Make sure you Define what the Right People should look like in skills, talents, abilities and attitudes and then agree to keep refining and retooling until a high-performing team emerges. Even having the Right People on your team will not guarantee success if your processes are broken.

Wrong Definitions Often Generate Confusion

Without exception, we have found that failed projects have one thing in common: poor, wrong or non-existent Definitions. Not having a clear Definition for "done" is a good example of this. Another is not having an explicit link to Vision, Purpose, Mission and/or the strategies of the organization. A lack of clear Definitions is an early indicator of eventual project failure. A high level of confusion can almost always be traced back to this root cause.

Wrong Definitions happen for many different reasons. For example, during the requirements gathering process, a team may either miss or omit requirements (functional or technical) that in the end may turn out to be key for completing the project. Many times, the end users do not fully understand or are unable to clearly communicate exactly what it is that they need, so requirements can be missed or poorly Defined.

Since requirements are not done in a vacuum, the teams can make the mistake of relying on trusted, existing business processes to come up with the Definitions for the project or product at hand. This could lead to waste since the team may have to rework or redefine their requirements if the original processes were ultimately broken or not suitable. Again, Definitions generated by poor processes usually result in confusion.

Another example of wrong Definitions includes creating unnecessary reports. Many project, program, product and portfolio leaders haven't realized the negative impact that unsuitable reports can have on their organization.

A key principle in lean is to find and eliminate waste. Lean thinking can be a powerful tool since it finds and eliminates process waste. Eliminating waste without impacting the operational productivity of the organization is the main objective.

> **NOT ENGAGING IN WASTED EFFORT IS ONE OF THE DIRECT BENEFITS OF BEING IN FLOW.**

For example, producing reports that no one reads or wants is a waste of time. We're not suggesting a one-size-fits-all strategy, either. A valuable report in one organization may be meaningless in another. A good leader will be able to identify which reports are relevant along with which ones can and should be eliminated. All reporting must be tailored to the culture and situation in which the organization is operating in order to reduce confusion and add value.

Another set of Definitions that you may want to create is an "enemies of adaptation" list. Items on this list could include processes, people, organizational dogmas, etc.

People and Resources Can Be an Anti-Flow

Many would agree that it is prudent to protect our sources of clean water as part of our collective obligation to be good stewards of our natural resources. Flow is the same since it enables good stewardship of the organization's natural resources. Since people and resources are limited in most organizations, they must be protected.

For example, in some cases it makes sense to group individuals into persistent dedicated teams. However, in other cases, pairing-up and rotating everyone through the organization makes sense. Having the wisdom to know when to use which tactic is one of the ways that Flow helps optimize the utilization of people and resources. People and resource allocation needs to be in alignment with Vision. A good example of the second type of resource allocation (of rotating everyone through the organization) is demonstrated by Menlo Innovations.

Richard Sheridan, Menlo's founder, describes how experts can be an impediment to innovation and Flow:

"The world certainly benefits from specialists, but unfortunately what happens in so many specialty practices is that the solution almost always fits the specialty, no matter the problem. Very few specialists have the capacity or the interest to step back and take a broader view." [102]

In other words, if all you have is a hammer, soon every problem looks like a nail.

Defining the skills, talents and abilities of the people needed to Deliver the organization's Vision is key to its success. Improper Definitions or poor agreements in this area will stifle Flow.

Wrong Distilled Agreements Often Produce Politics

Assumptions are clearly the enemy of Flow. It is almost universal when we train around the world to find project or product Delivery teams making major assumptions and then beginning execution without having done the hard work of creating clear Definitions and Distilling the agreements needed for successful Delivery. Lack of clarity in Definitions means that all relevant agreements are flawed. If the agreements are flawed, you will either end up with an incomplete or completely undesirable outcome. When this occurs – and it will occur – the net result, organizationally, is politics.

By politics we mean an attention to secondary agendas and/or tribal warfare between the various internal entities. Fractures occur because the focus shifts from the overarching True Vision to political skirmishes. Politics are never fully avoided, but clear Definitions and Distilled agreements remove most of these anti-patterns.

One of the most neglected areas of Distillation is the prioritization of projects. It is not uncommon for us to find organizations, which hire us as external consultants, to be overcommitted by 200 to 300 percent. This problem is caused by poor Distillation. Prioritization generally looks this way: Which of these projects is a number one priority? Answer: All of them. When presented with the brutal fact that team capacity will not Deliver the current scheduled work it is usually a difficult and not always successful discussion. However, gaining agreement on prioritization is absolutely necessary. Without proper authority, this process can take months. Forcing prioritization is the same thing as cutting up the credit cards for someone who is addicted to shopping. It may not be pretty, but it is essential to fiscal health. Prioritization, in a healthy organization, is iterative and ongoing.

It is also good to remember that "perfect" can be the enemy of "done," especially when you are trying to get a product out the door. Perhaps the 80/20 rule applies here, too. If the product meets 80% of the customer's needs, then ship it. Unless, of course, the customer is paying for or needs a perfect product, service or result. There are some products where 80% may result in the death of the end user. So, clearly in those cases, we do not use the 80/20 rule.

But, most products or services simply do not fall into the life or death category. And, most products can be iteratively improved over time and the customer, in most cases, is willing to wait for the perfection to emerge over time.

The work needed for any agreement of value should be Distilled and decided at the last responsible moment, but as early as what is prudent in the process.

Wrong Delivery Creates Chaos

Once you have your Definitions and have Distilled agreement, you can begin to iteratively Deliver. Without fail, regardless of methodology used, you will encounter an "oh, by the way" from a stakeholder or customer that just realized that they forgot to include a Definition from the start. When that happens, and it will, you need to then filter this "oh, by the way" with the lens of the Vision for the product or project, since you now have an altered project. This alteration could be slight or massive, but it should still be focused on Delivering the Vision regardless of the change.

If this iterative step (of returning to Definitions, filtering the new requirement or change and, if included, then a new Distillation of agreement) is missed, your Delivery could fail. If there are politics involved, be aware that a stakeholder may have an agenda that is not in alignment with the Vision of the product or project. Maintaining a focus on the True Vision helps keep secondary agendas in check.

We have observed that there is no better way to impede or hamper a work effort than to introduce confusion and chaos into the work process by assuming that the True Vision is being followed.

The first example of confusion spinning a project off the table is thousands of years old. It is the story about the Tower of Babel. We unpack this story in "The Nehemiah Effect." It is from that story that we Distilled the One Language + One Mind + One Plan = One Vision formula. The Tower of Babel, being the negative application of the powerful use of this formula.

When Definitions are not understood, or agreed to via Distillation, then achieving One Language is not possible. Everyone will do what is right in his or her own eyes and so attaining one mind and Delivering the proposed plan becomes difficult or impossible.

Maintaining focus and agreement is really the work required at the leadership level. Without this effort, chaos ensues. It also includes the work needed to identify and Deliver the Cascading "one thing" mentioned earlier.

Even when the work of strong Definitions, agreement and the planning is done well, you can still end up with chaos and confusion. This is particularly true in very large projects that have multiple cross dependencies and integration points. We have found over and over again the importance of keeping all of the work, regardless of the size to the project, in a big and visual format. Having a tangible, big picture is a good starting point for eliminating chaos and confusion. It is also a tool that helps the leadership team maintain the focus and agreement.

When possible, we use a war room.

We seldom make it complex.

Complexity is easy to drift into if one is not careful. In the same way, it is important to keep all of your tools simple and light. For example, we have found that PMOs or Portfolio Directors that focus on tool normalization are usually focusing on proxy variables instead of confronting and addressing the real issues. This is one of the primary reasons that PMOs fail to Deliver on their promise and value-add. So, when Andrew was on an assignment at NPG he spent the first two years testing and throwing out many tools that some stakeholders wanted the PMO to use. Those tools ended up demonstrating that they could not add any tangible value to what the leadership was trying to achieve.

This does not mean that tools are bad. A great example of the successful use of a simple tool to track hours (which is considered an absolute anti-pattern in most Agile circles) is used at Menlo Innovations. They project and track hours on a physical chart each week. The team constructs it and the client agrees to it. This allows them to accurately invoice their clients without the potential drama that relative estimations can create.

However, the tracking of hours, in many cultures, is a punitive exercise used by management to try to increase individual productivity. Tracking hours in this way is another example of a proxy variable. Menlo does not use hours in this way. The other difference with Menlo's system is that they can accurately project real costs for projects. Many Agile purists bristle at the thought of hour tracking and forecasting. Menlo has proven in a pure Agile environment that both can be done without harm to the employees or customer relationships.

If you have faulty Definitions and poor agreements, it is impossible to have a strong Delivery plan, which only results in chaos and/or confusion. A high performing organization that is operating in Flow will experience the same market and environmental disruptions that every organization experiences. But, they will find the creative, innovation solutions to successfully navigate any challenge that rises as they Drive towards fulfilling their Vision. Timothy Rowe, founder of Cambridge Incubator, states:

"A lot of problems in business are not because the CEO doesn't have the right values. It's because the CEO isn't effective at communicating them throughout the entire organization." [103]

Effective Delivery requires a good plan and effective communication.

Wrong Drive Generates Division

Driving the organization based on command-and-control focus on production or profitability alone is an anti-Flow. The focus or Vision needs to be on a higher Purpose or more compelling "WHY" if it is going to succeed as an organizational driver.

"Failure to understand this conundrum – that satisfaction depends not merely on having goals, but having the right goals – can lead sensible people down self-destructive paths. If people chase profit goals, reach those goals, and still don't feel any better about their lives, one response is to increase the size and scope of the goals-to seek more money or outside validation. And that can 'drive them down a road of further unhappiness thinking it's the road to happiness…'" [104]

A culture of fear anti-pattern fosters division. Many times, shame and/or guilt are used as a motivator. But the reality is that fear, shame and guilt demotivate and kill Flow:

"Fear prompts retreat. It is the antipode of progress." [105]
STEVEN KOTLER WITH PETER DIAMANDIS

In a fear-based culture, failure is seldom accepted and almost never encouraged. This obviously stifles innovation and creativity that are the necessary fuel for achieving continuous improvement and always a vital part of high-performance.

The antidote to fear is a fearless mindset or approach. This does not happen by default. It requires intention:

"Fearlessness is like a muscle: the more we use it, the stronger it becomes. The more we are willing to risk failure and act on our dreams and our desires, the more fearless we become and the easier it is the next time. Bottom line, taking risks is an indispensable part of any creative act" [106]

Why Some Retrospectives Fail to Drive Success

A retrospective is an intentional time box set aside to look at and think through ways to get better as a team or organization. When done correctly, it is a powerful tool that drives innovation and continuous improvement:

"Implementing continuous self-improvement requires a fundamentally different kind of mindset from traditional management. It involves creating an environment in which the organization draws on the full talents and capacities of the people who work there. It means generating a context in which workers want to improve and are given the means to do so, so that they do evolve into a high-performance mode. It's about powering up the internal energy of teams so that they transcend their limitations and create products or services that generate client delight." [107]

STEVEN DENNING

Many studies have shown that, regardless of the type of Agile approach used, almost half of Agile teams do not use retrospectives. We believe that this is because the teams were never trained in effective retrospective facilitation. Or, they do not fully understand the power these meetings release or fully see the value. Other times it is the result of senior management not understanding the value and/or not wanting the team to waste time on the activity, thus preventing the teams from allocating the necessary time. Finally, we rarely find any team actually performing retrospectives using Vision as the lens. If the retrospective is not filtered through the lens of the True Vision, then it can be rendered meaningless even if it is conducted. Obviously, the organization loses in all of the above scenarios.

Even teams conducting retrospectives can fall into a rut of "he said-she said" finger pointing and thus not focusing on true, continuous team or organizational self-improvement. Steven Denning observes that high-performing retrospectives require a particular mindset:

"Continuous self-improvement is not a bunch of low-level production techniques to eliminate waste at the factory level. It's a deeply rooted set of values and attitudes focused on fixing problems as soon as they occur." [108]

Another reason that we have found that retrospectives fail to Deliver the intended value, is when teams focus on proxy variables instead of Vision. Maintaining a focus on Vision is not the natural default mode for anyone apart from the person holding the ultimate Vision. Because of this truism, teams will focus on the functional aspects of the project or increment on which they are working.

If their effort is focused on improved cycle time, for example, and the improvement does not Deliver value for the True Vision, then it is a proxy variable. If it does Deliver value, then focusing on cycle time is a true variable. Spending time improving proxy variables is oscillating, not truly iterating and can lead to unproductive or failed retrospectives. Retrospectives, done well, help eliminate division and point teams to higher levels of productivity.

At an Enterprise level, an excellent tool for retrospectives for determining team and organizational health are a set of radars from Sally Elatta and her team (see http://agilityhealthradar.com/radars/) available from Agile Transformations Inc. The Growth Items that are a result of the Team Radar Retrospective, for example, can be narrowed down to one or two items, that when addressed by senior and executive management will help facilitate the feedback loop on the left side of our Cascading VSPT and "one thing" chart shared earlier. We are in the final stages of adding a Flow Health Radar to Sally's set.

Not all Anti-patterns are "Anti-patterns"

One of the most powerful and useful tools in successful Agile environments is making the Vision and all of the work big and visible. Not having the Vision and work big and visible would then appear to be an anti-pattern. However, circumstances do not always allow this. A perfect example of a situation where none of the work can be made visible on a wall or whiteboard is inside a submarine.

This is the situation that Captain David Marquet was facing when he assumed command of the Santa Fe. In "Turn the Ship Around" he shares the verbal processes and practices he used to make the Vision central to operation of the ship and also how he moved decision making to the lowest responsible level, in a highly Agile fashion. For many Agile purists, this presents a conundrum since not having visible artifacts or information radiators in the team space reduces team effectiveness. One of the most powerful things he did was to push authority from his chair to the submarine chiefs. Chiefs on a submarine are basically equivalent to the team leaders in an Agile environment. Once the authority was Delivered and accepted, performance improved exponentially, as we shared in Chapter 3 in the section on "Getting to Aha!"

Two more anti-patterns that we have encountered that ended-up not being anti-patters is the use of Project Managers and tracking time in an Agile environment. Menlo Innovations is a brilliant example of both of these being used successfully in a fully Agile shop (as we share above in the anti-Flow section for "Deliver").

We have recently begun to understand that another holy grail of Agile team areas – open and transparent environments – is not necessarily required for optimal team performance and may actually reduce performance. Susan Cain, in her work regarding introverts, found that open spaces are an obstacle and anti-pattern (as an absolute solution) for an introvert to achieve personal high-performance:

"It's also vital to recognize that many people – especially introverts like Steve Wozniak – need extra quiet and privacy in order to do their best work.

Some companies are beginning to understand the value of silence and solitude, and are creating 'flexible' open plans that offer a mix of solo workspaces, quiet zones, casual meeting areas, cafés, reading rooms, computer hubs, and even 'streets' where people can chat casually with each other without interrupting other's workflow.

These kinds of diverse workspaces benefit introverts as well as extroverts." [109]

Another anti-pattern is taking the idea of anti-patterns too far.

For example, recently a Kanban trainer tweeted out that he was banning the word "task" from all of his Kanban training and coaching. That's his prerogative, but we will continue to use the phrase "task" in our training, coaching and mentoring. Managing tasks and time is not the enemy nor is it an anti-pattern. Tasks need to be accomplished for work to be done.

Back in 1984 the idea of work as a prioritized backlog already existed (the prioritized daily task list) when the first Franklin Day Planner was introduced to the world. The task list was re-prioritized by the user every day (should sound familiar to most Agilists). However, the history of the idea of prioritization stretches even further back than that. Great leaders down through the ages have all used similar methodologies to get things done. For example, Dwight D.

Eisenhower used the following prioritization system to separate the important from the not important and the urgent from the not urgent:

DO *(IMPORTANT AND URGENT)*
DECIDE *(IMPORTANT BUT NOT URGENT)*
DELEGATE *(NOT IMPORTANT BUT URGENT)*
DELETE *(NEITHER IMPORTANT NOR URGENT)*

Our best guess is that the former President of the United States was using his system (at least he's given credit for it) long before he became president back in 1953. Franklin Quest went on to include a similar idea to Eisenhower's approach in his task and time management system called the Franklin Day Planner— dedicated to and named after Benjamin Franklin's time management system that he developed during his lifetime in the 1700s.

The Franklin system incorporates Eisenhower's prioritization method so that tasks are prioritized by A (Do), B (Delegate) and C (Decide). "D" (Delete) items didn't even make the list, which is a very powerful lean concept for eliminating wasteful activities and tasks. The single, most powerful part of lean is eliminating waste in the value chain. Eisenhower's and Franklin's systems are a great way to do exactly that. Task lists are not nearly as effective as PostIt® notes on a Kanban board, but they have had their place and many people still use them effectively.

Franklin's system is just one example of a simple, disciplined, easy to use time and task management framework that links your daily tasks to your personal and business Vision, Mission, Goals and Objectives. Any system like this will help you be successful in achieving and realizing your overall Vision and Goals.

This may be why some people from the business side of an organization scratch their heads when the Technology and IT teams are so over-the-top enthusiastic about Agile and want them to start using it as well. In their minds, as successful business leaders, they have already been using and/or implementing the similar ideas to "agile" and "lean" thinking. The Franklin system, Goldmine, SalesForce.com, or similar tools, have been used for decades. All of these systems, to one degree or another, break down break down Vision, epics, capabilities and features down to the task level. They use other labels, but the same ideas are all contained in those systems.

The problem with the successful use of any tool or method is that it can blind the people using it to other alternatives. Their success causes them to dismiss voices from other tribes. While there are many practices and methods found in Agile, Scrum and Flow that can help accelerate individuals and teams to a higher-level of success, regardless of current methodologies, without the work of unifying around a simple framework and language, organizational high-performance may be limited.

To do lists, without clear Vision and singular focus, tend to become a clutter of activity, regardless of how successful they are at Delivering value for some people. Gary Keller says it this way:

"It seems that everywhere we turn we're encouraged to make lists --- and though lists are invaluable, they have a dark side. While to-dos serve as a useful collection of our best intentions, they also tyrannize us with trivial, unimportant stuff that we feel obligated to get done --- because it is on our list.

If allowed, they set our priorities the same way an inbox can dictate our day. The things which are most important don't always scream the loudest.

To-do lists inherently lack the intent of success. In fact, most to-do lists are actually just survival lists --- getting you through your day and life, but not making each day a stepping stone for the next so that you sequentially build a successful life. To-do lists tend to be long; success lists are short. One pulls you in all directions; the other aims you in a specific direction.[110]

We believe that all work effort needs Distillation of Vision down to the people and tasks. Without clear and agreed to Definitions at the task level, you are pulled in multiple directions and confusion will result.

At the task level, we advocate using a stripped-down, personal Kanban board to control personal WIP (work-in-process) at the task level. You can create this on your desk by using blue masking tape to create a T-pattern. Put your most pressing "to do" items (PostIt® notes) on the left and "done" items on the right. Some people include a middle column for "doing" items. Feel free to experiment and use what works best for your work flow.

One of our Flow Certified Professionals (FCP), during the FCP training session, observed that Flow is a values-based framework unlike other rules-based methodologies that are top-heavy and monolithic. Flow is light, easy to communicate and will always increase performance.

Organizations are only as successful as the collective achievements of each and every individual in that organization, rolled-up to Deliver the Vision. If team members can't prioritize and Deliver what is most important and valuable to their project or workflow in their daily work, then the odds for failure at the organizational level remain quite high.

Achieving a state of Flow is both an art and a science. It includes the disciplined pursuit of personal and organizational excellence. Everyone wants to be on a winning team in a healthy culture. Moreover, teams that have the right habits – including the pursuit of excellence in how to Deliver their personal and team work effort – are the ones that win. Having the entire organization operate at the same cadence using the same language focused on Delivery of the Vision is the path to the Cascading domino effect of exponential results. It doesn't happen overnight and requires disciplined focus to achieve it.

This is how Aristotle describes achieving a state of high-performing Flow:

"Excellence is an art won by training and habituation. We do not act rightly because we have virtue or excellence, but we rather have those because we have acted rightly. We are what we repeatedly do. Excellence, then, is not an act but a habit."

So, what is the point?

Our "task-free" Kanban friend, mentioned earlier, has not magically eliminated "tasks" by eliminating the use of the word. People still have to do tasks to Deliver value. Work still has to happen. Renaming "tasks" does not alter the work that has to be done. You have simply relabeled it.

If it works better for you to find a substitute for the word "task," then, by all means, feel free to do so. However, make sure that the entire organization understands and agrees with the change before instituting it. We don't think that you actually need to ban the use of the word "task." But, if you do, do so carefully and with agreement.

A small word of advice to our Agile friends: banning the use of a word like "task" with tenacious, religious zeal can quickly kill your (and the Agile community's) credibility and cause organizational leadership to roll their eyes. Worse yet, because it is such an inane distinction, it can detract from what you are trying to accomplish with Agile.

If you are going to change labels, the use of humor is often an effective communication tool. For example, a recent client had named one of their backlogs the "*'crap'* list." Well, they actually used a rougher version of the same word, but you get the point. It was a clear label that effectively and quickly communicated to everyone.

One anti-pattern that should go on everyone's "*'crap'* list" is when managers add features or more projects to a system that is over capacity. This does not speed up production, it slows it down. The formula for this is Cycle Time = Throughput divided by Work-in-process. This is known in engineering circles as Little's Law.

The examples shared above remind us that conversations about anti-patterns are far from over. While we have not taken the time to research it, we are fast coming to the conclusion that for every anti-pattern there is probably a stunning example that contradicts the anti-pattern. This creates an issue and potential blocker since some in the Agile community treat certain anti-patterns as if they were core religious beliefs and react with pious zeal to eliminate them or anyone who opposes their doctrines. Doing this is, in and of itself, an anti-pattern and also can create an anti-Flow. Sometimes iterative improvements may violate core Agile beliefs and yet succeed in a particular situation or culture. We should embrace and affirm this success, as long as it is Delivering the Vision and the "one thing."

Chapter 7

Disrupted Flow

To help the reader better understand what we're trying to communicate from the examples of anti-patterns in chapter 6, we would like to share the following example from the world of sports:

Agile Madness

What is Agile Madness?

And, what does it have to do with Flow?

Or, Vision and Culture?

We will get to that in a bit.

First a little bit of context.

Our use of the idea of Flow mirrors the sports world. All of the Kallman brothers (there are four of us) played basketball at the High School and College levels.

Our dad loved basketball.

He refereed high school games, coached YMCA teams and was a co-owner and eventual general manager of the semi-pro basketball team, the Lansing Capitals, back in the late 1960s and early 1970s. Dad was also President of the Upper Peninsula Club of Lansing that hosted the annual Sunday morning breakfast for all of the Upper Peninsula teams that made it down to Lansing to play in the Statewide High School basketball semi-finals and finals.

We believe that you get the point.

We were a basketball family.

March Madness enters full swing in the US every March.

It is the month when the NCAA men's basketball tournament occurs and millions of people pay close attention as the 68 selected teams wind their way to the final-four weekend and eventual championship game. With over 80 million brackets filled out, it causes a lot of conversations and a fair amount of lost time at work.

For those who actually follow sports, you are likely aware that there has been an ongoing debate about the effective use of statistics to improve team performance. For example, in basketball, the percentage of shots taken to the percentage of shots missed, from what position on the floor, by which player, etc. are used by coaches to understand individual performance.

However, knowing an individual's performance statistics (like "tracking hours" on team members for a project) does not automatically improve performance. Inappropriate use of statistics can actually reduce performance. Focusing on statistics does not necessarily create a high-performing team or achieve the championship results in sports. It is a proxy variable.

Statistics are important, but they don't tell the whole story.

Some organizations seem to think that statistics are the "holy grail" of management. For example, we continuously get pushback from large, corporate clients when we suggest doing away with the time tracking of team member's hours (except for resource management or tracking a consultant's billable hours). Measuring individual effort using hours has been proven, over and over, to be an anti-pattern to high-performing teams. Menlo tracks hours by team, not by individual.

Large organizations, particularly the finance arm, want to know individual effort as described by hours spent. They typically want to normalize Agile "story points" by using hours as the metric. You will even find hours as a checkbox within many of the large Agile Enterprise tools.

Why? Because the finance leaders want to see hours reported, so hours it is.

However, they don't understand that data is just a rear-view mirror. Measuring hours will give you information, but it will not give you high-performance. It can be useful and predictive (to a point), but tracking data does not inspire change. Leadership and the human factor must be considered.

High-performing teams are led by coaches who understand how to create and maintain a state of Flow for the team. Management, seeing the outstanding results realized by a particular Agile team, then want to export those same results to other teams in the organization.

From a management perspective, it is the old "you cannot manage what you cannot measure." So, management needs to recognize that focusing only on statistics can be a blocker to high-performance.

However, combining statistics with leadership to deliver an amazing result was demonstrated well in the movie "Money Ball" with Brad Pitt. Pitt was playing the role of Billy Beane, the general manager of the Oakland Athletics baseball team. Billy used statistics to select specific skills to build the team strategically with very little money. But, the Oakland A's did not become a high-performing team just because they were using statistics to determine which players to add to their roster. They achieved high-performance with the people chosen through leadership and team dynamics. An example of that in the movie is where Billy chats with an older player and says, "I need you to lead." That player decided to step up and his leadership helped the team to gel and move into a state of Flow. That led to a championship, a completely unexpected result.

A more recent example is the Tri-Unity Christian High School (Wyoming, Michigan) boys' varsity basketball team during the 2015 season. Tri-Unity had won the district finals every year for the past 20+ years in Class D. They have also been to the semi-finals and finals multiple times, and they have won the state championship twice. They are used to winning. However, they started the 2014-15 season with only 4 wins and 9 losses. The center on their team, Chris Osantowski, a 6' 8" (203 cm) senior, was performing well below his potential during that opening stretch.

It was at this point that the assistant coach, Bob Przybysz, had a chat with him. The discussion did not focus on the ups and downs of basketball. Instead, Bob talked with him about his Vision of becoming a youth pastor and impacting the world for Christ. Bob continued to paint a picture of the platform that could be created by young people looking up to a young man who played basketball well, but also had a passion for God.

From that point forward, Chris' game performance went up dramatically, inspiring the rest of the team in the process, and Tri-Unity went on to win 11 of the next 12 games, until finally losing in that year's State quarterfinals. It wasn't the tracking of individual or team performance statistics that brought about this change; it was the clear focus on Vision combined with the Distillation of agreement based on a personal, white-hot WHY that created the radical change and outstanding results individually. This personal transformation also resulted in moving the entire team into a high-performing state. They entered a state of Flow.

We have seen the same thing repeated hundreds of times in both corporate and non-profit organizational environments. The focus needs to be on Vision. And when that is clear and everybody agrees, results are exponential. By the way, nobody tracked the number of hours invested in practice before or after Tri-Unity's transformation during that basketball season. Tracking of statistics gives useful information, but does not move teams or organizations into a state of Flow.

"You will get what you measure" is a true statement, but measuring hours is a proxy variable. Knowing the amount of time of spent on any particular task, (e.g., how much time was spent practicing), does not magically cause the speed at which future tasks are completed to improve. Even if the tasks are done more quickly, that does not necessarily increase the odds of successfully reaching the ultimate goal.

Tracking hours does not Deliver high performance.

The belief that tracking hours will somehow supernaturally Deliver high performance is what we now call "Agile Madness." This is an unreasonable expectation. Expecting to achieve exceptional results using an anti-pattern is madness. This is also a perfect example of blending some Agile practices with an anti-pattern, relabeling it "Agile;" and, then blaming "Agile" when it fails.

We should be measuring things that show progress toward achieving the goal. A clear, True Vision thus becomes the ultimate, or true, key performance indicator (KPI). All KPIs used by any executive or manager should link to Vision and align the organization to successfully Deliver the Vision. Any unlinked measurement is an anti-pattern and waste. And, it may potentially disrupt the Flow of the team.

The 2004 US Olympic Basketball team demonstrates how disrupted Flow crippled the best talent on the planet and rendered the team impotent:

"There were some top players on that team – LeBron James, Tim Duncan, Alan Iverson, to name just a few – and the United States had a history of not only winning but dominating in the sport, particularly since professional players had been allowed to participate. The American basketball players knew they were the best. Except that they weren't. They lost more games than any US Olympic basketball team had ever lost. They lost to Lithuania. Their pride and complacency were their downfall. They were living in a happy bubble." [111]

JEFF SUTHERLAND

Living in a happy bubble does not Deliver high-performance, even when high-performing individuals are brought together as a team. The elements of Flow are still needed to Deliver exceptional results. Flow plus high-performing individuals equals hyper-performing results. Leadership is more important than statistics:

"The role of a leader is not to come up with all of the great ideas. The role of a leader is to create an environment in which great ideas can happen." [112]

SIMON CINEK

The environment is what most people refer to as "Culture." Creating the right Culture (or environment) takes Vision, a clear Mission, a Purpose or white hot why, and a Cascading "one thing," as well as the continuous visibility and verbal encouragement to that end. Without the right Culture, even the best people in the world will not deliver the hoped-for results; and, great ideas will never rise. A toxic Culture will guarantee poor results, regardless of skill, talent and ability.

SECTION 4:

CONCLUSION AND APPENDICES

Chapter 8

Training, Coaching and Mentoring

Three of the key enablers for reaching optimal performance are training, coaching and mentoring. And, being able to work across the spectrum of methodologies is one of the reasons Flow is so effective.

We believe value can be derived from all methodologies.

Consider the following sports metaphor.

During the 1980's Andrew participated in Tae Kwon Do for seven years and European Kickboxing for four years after that. He also learned the basics of Aikido, Judo and Kung Fu.

Mr. Kim, his Tae Kwon Do (TKD) instructor from the Michigan State University TKD club was originally from Korea. In order to get a black belt in TKD from Mr. Kim, he insisted that all his students learn both the traditional and modern styles of TKD.

One might ask, "wasn't the modern style enough?"

Well, not really.

The following example illustrates this point:

Every now and then the MSU TKD club would have a sparing competition with other clubs in the Lansing, Michigan area. Another club, with which we had a "friendly" rivalry, brought nothing but black belts to a competition. Andrew was only a blue belt at that time. Mr. Kim said, "Andrew, you're first up. Oh, by the way, the other guy is a 2nd degree black belt." Andrew looked at Mr. Kim as if he had lost his mind, but Mr. Kim knew that a blue belt from his team could easily defeat a 2nd degree black belt from any other club. Andrew won with a TKO (technical knockout) in less than two minutes. It was only a semi-contact tournament. But, Andrew accidentally knocked the wind completely out of the black belt.

We should back-up a little and set some context for those that may not be familiar with TKD or martial arts in general. There is no one more dangerous in TKD than a yellow or blue belt. They have mastered the basics of all of the techniques, but don't necessarily have full control over execution. Mr. Kim regularly shared a story with his students about the wife of a MSU football player that had just earned her yellow belt. Her husband was a rather large and very strong individual. He was teasing her and asked, "What would you do if I attacked you like this?" And he made the mistake of rushing at her. Without even thinking, her training kicked-in and she executed a perfect sidekick to his privates. Her kick was executed so perfectly that she ended up sending him to the emergency room at the local hospital for treatment.

Back to Andrew's sparing match.

The black belt opponent executed a "modern" attack. Andrew without thinking, dropped down into an old-school (read: waterfall), deep-stance counter-attack that literally lifted the black belt off the ground with a single punch. The pained and shocked expression on the face of the black belt said it all as he flew backwards through the air with his hands and feet trailing after his body. The punch was so effortless that Andrew didn't even feel the contact.

After the tournament, Andrew was chatting with the black belt and apologized for the "full-contact" hit. The black belt accepted his apology and remarked, "I've never been punched that hard in my entire life."

"Tradition" quickly triumphed over "modern" that day.

The black belt's club only taught a modern style of TKD that was considered state-of-the-art at that time. However, Mr. Kim wisely taught both modern and traditional TKD. The MSU club won every match in the tournament, hands down. And, it didn't matter if it was a blue, brown or black belt from the MSU club that was matched up against the other club's first, second or third degree black belts. Modern techniques, by themselves, were not enough to beat someone that was trained in both the old and new styles.

Mr. Kim urged his students to pursue a complete fighting style. This included learning a wrestling style, such as Judo or Greco-Roman wrestling. He also had them learn Hapkido (the Korean version of Aikido) where you incorporated self-defense moves like wristlocks, etc.

This was demonstrated by Mr. Kim's own pedigree. He was a black belt in TKD as well as a black belt/expert in Judo (a coach for the US Olympic Judo team), Hapkido and Kendo (bamboo sword fighting --- since a complete fighter will have also mastered the use of at least one weapon).

He had a complete fighting system and was an excellent teacher, coach and mentor since he shared with (and modeled for) his students what they needed to do in order to have an all-encompassing fighting methodology.

The same concept applies to organizational leadership.

There are a lot of people from the traditional side of the table that don't really get Agile or Scrum, and vice versa. That is why we view all project and organizational management as a continuum from traditional at the one end to Agile at the other. If you are not competent in all methodologies, then you probably do not have a complete project, program, portfolio or organizational management "style" and you are at risk of being at the receiving end of an unexpected body blow delivered by a well-trained yellow belt.

In our mind, it is not enough to only understand the modern, "Agile" way of working and then assume that you have the best fighting style. This could not be further from the truth. The reality is that a majority of people do not work in companies like Spotify, Google, et al, that are considered 100 percent "Agile." Most people work in either a Traditional or a blended environment. It would be wise to understand how to work and succeed in all types of settings. And, occasionally, you need to know how to throw the right punch at the right time using the right style.

We have leveraged the wisdom of learning both traditional and modern styles in many organizations. We try to make sure that all ScrumMasters (modern style) are trained in traditional Project Management (old style), much to their dismay. Likewise, we have all of the project managers learn Agile methods and practices.

Lifelong learning is foundational to the personal pursuit of excellence. Learning does not stop when you finish school. It also doesn't stop once you have an FCP, FCT, AHF, PMP, PMI-ACP, CSM, CSP, CST, ITIL, Prince2 or whatever other certification you might have added to your personal toolkit. Learning never stops and never should.

We are personally committed to lifelong learning. We encourage individuals, teams and organizations to do the same. Once people are trained, the process doesn't stop there. Implementing a framework doesn't happen all by itself. It requires experienced coaches and mentors that have "been there, done that." Sure, you can read a book (like this one) and immediately begin to implement what you *think* you have learned. But, more often than not, there is a significant value-add to having coaches and mentors with the right skill and experience to guide you safely through the mind fields of implementation. And, to teach you how to deliver the right punch, at the right time, in the right spot.

Part of this learning, as we have mentioned before, includes understanding the difference between the language of leadership and the language of management.

Executives are not going to waste their time with an Agile Coach who doesn't speak their language or is unfamiliar with their space. So, if an Agile Coach (unencumbered by knowledge or experience) communicates poorly with an executive in a meeting, then the coach probably will never be invited back to the table. Worse yet, we have observed that some Agile Coaches, who have experienced this removal, wear it as a badge of honor. Whenever this happens, it drives another nail in the coffin for anyone attempting to scale the success of team-level Agile to higher levels in an organization. Many self-labeled Enterprise Agile coaches make the rookie mistake of assuming that all you need to do is replicate team-level Agile processes at the higher organizational levels and, voilà, suddenly everyone is "Agile" everywhere in the organization. This ignores the fact that Vision and leadership are functional realities as you move up the organization chart. Team-level Agile needs to reflect the Vision, but it does not organically create the Vison. Failure to recognize this is a sure harbinger of failure.

Agile practices and principles can be applied to leadership team cultures, but it is a different environment than street-level, operational Delivery. To scale any Agile system, you need to Define and Deliver value, not just reproduce or optimize processes alone. Flow is how we Define and Deliver remarkable value at the Enterprise-level.

The Vision and Mission should embody your organization's white-hot WHY and "one thing." Passion and excellence that is not led by a clear Purpose will eventually fizzle out, regardless of the skill of the person coaching. It will simply not be sustainable.

Vision is always the driver.

If the leadership of an organization is merely talking the talk and not walking the talk, then all of the effort and investment in creating a Vision and the Strategies for achieving that Vision will be wasted. The organization's stated core Values and attitudes are only as real as each and every leader's daily walk:

> *"Every well-run organization has not only a good business plan, but a set of core values that are expressed in the behavior of the leadership and are continuously reinforced through written statements and verbal communication."* [113]

MIHALY CSIKSZENTMIHALYI

Core values are not organically grown from the bottom-up. They are established and lived by leaders. Trainers, coaches and mentors can provide incredibly useful feedback to an organization's leadership regarding "blind spots" or organizational gaps. But it still comes back around to the Culture created by leaders.

Recently Andrew attended a leadership conference where one of the presenters shared research that the average number of blind spots that an individual has is 3.4. So, if you have a team of eight people working together, then it is likely you are facing 27 blind spots to manage. While we don't have any concrete evidence, we suspect that blind spots probably operate exponentially.

At the individual level, if you personally don't think that you have "3.4 blind spots," then check with your spouse or close friend and ask them. Better yet, ask your mother-in-law or children. By the way, if you are not able to accept feedback regarding personal blind spots, then you are going to have a tough time accepting or receiving feedback in your business environment. It is also unlikely that you will be able to conduct difficult discussions related to blind spots with your team members or other organizational stakeholders.

Every organization has its fair share of blind spots to manage. When organizations or individuals are operating in a state of Flow, blind spots tend to become visible quickly and many times painfully. When exposed, these blind spots can be eliminated or mitigated; but, sometimes the pain created by the needed change causes the organization to withdraw. Again, servant leadership is needed and if it is not present the organization will revert quickly to old habits and ways of working.

We believe that blind spots are the reason many companies that have started out attempting to be completely Agile are struggling to remain Agile as they grow into larger, more mature enterprises. The heartburn usually tends to manifest itself somewhere around the 500 to 700 employee level. We have witnessed that one well known, highly regarded, "poster-child" Agile start-up actually brought in PMP Certified trainers to teach the basics of traditional project management to its organization. The idea of the continuum found a home with them and we anticipate that it will help this organization perform even better.

Flow enables leaders to more effectively manage intangibles like blind spots, passion, strategies, etc. The simple elegance of Flow is that it spans the gap between abstract and concrete. And it enables the white-hot WHY and the "one thing" from the executive office to be Delivered by the task-level decisions of every person involved. The Flow formula is simple:

Vision + Right People + the 4D Model = Successful Organization

Simple is not easy to do, especially when you have to do it simultaneously in the "I, We, It and Its" boxes of the organization. The case studies included at the end of this book utilize the above formula to demonstrate the power of Flow regardless of where it is applied.

Chapter 9

Conclusion

B y now, we hope you can see how Flow benefits individuals, products and organizations. When the elements of Flow are properly woven together, it Delivers outstanding results.

If you remember, our beginning Definition of Flow was:

"The state of optimal performance achieved by applying a clear, consistent, persistent and unified Vision at all levels of an organization."

Our ending Definition of Flow is now simply:

"The optimal state of high performance."

For Flow to be realized, it is essential to have the Right People at every level. Also, everybody needs to come to work with an intrinsic, burning passion to be even better than the day before. This level of excellence can only be achieved by knowing what your, your team's and your organization's white-hot WHY and "one thing" are. J. Irwin Miller, CEO of Cummins Engines once said:

"You have to create an atmosphere in which people want to give their best. You don't order anyone to do their best. You couldn't order Beethoven to compose the Ninth Symphony. He's got to want to do it. And so the head of a business is an enabler rather than a doer." [114]

Mihaly Csikszentmihalyi followed this thought a few pages later with:

"It's impossible to create an environment that will foster flow without commitment from top management. Leadership must embrace the idea that before products, profit, and market share they are primarily responsible for the emotional well-being of their workers." [115]

At an individual level, to operate in Flow, you need to understand and know what your personal white-hot WHY and "one thing" are and how that relates to your team, division and organization's True Vision. If this is not in place, work needs to be done to get there.

At a team level, Scrum and Agile are exploding in large part because they can Deliver all the elements for successful Flow. However, clarity of Vision and the Cascading "one thing" (and VSPT) do not happen by chance. Both require conscious effort and hard work. If this work has not been done at the team level, organizational dissonance and failure may ensue.

Do not assume that following the principles and practices of Scrum or any other Agile methodology will automatically create the environment necessary for Flow to exist or for exponential results to occur. It is not an "either/or" but rather a "both/and." The communication of a team's white-hot WHY and "one thing" still require leadership and still need to be linked to the higher Purpose of the organizational Vision. We believe that the 58 percent failure rate experienced by Scrum and Agile team-level efforts are more than likely attributable to this.

"Without vision, flexibility is just an abstraction. It is a measure of what we could do if we ever got the gumption to try it (be we haven't and we won't)." [116]

TOM DEMARCO

The same is true for your product, services or results.

An organization's programs, processes and portfolios need to Flow from the heart of a clearly understood and cogently communicated white-hot WHY and "one thing." Lining up the first two-inch domino, aimed in the right direction, will eventually explode into amazing results. And, as things rapidly change in the market, environment, or Culture, adjustments and adaptations can be done quickly and profitably.

The ultimate state of Flow for an organization is when all of the teams and individuals are unified and operating in their own state of Flow. Trust must be established and lived at every level or Flow will break down with diminished results. You cannot give what you do not own. By establishing and giving trust, the organization acquires trust. This is effective from your point of leadership down. You can enable down but only influence up.

Our desire is that your business or project accelerates to stunning, lightning fast results. And, that it surpasses what even the visionary leader of your organization thought you could Deliver. To be massively creative in the face of volatile circumstances that could not have been anticipated a short time ago.

For instance:

"Forty-three percent of IBM's revenue last year came from products not possible two years ago." [117]

DANIEL BURRUS

Volatility is now the norm. Daniel Burrus in his excellent book, "Flash Foresight" talks at length about the necessity to identify and align with the clear hard trends of the obvious future. He says:

"Agility has been quite a buzzword lately in corporate circles … 'the competition and the marketplace are changing so fast, everything's is changing so fast, that if you want to survive, you need to be incredibly agile …' In the twenty-first century, being proactive has outlived its usefulness. It's too late to be proactive: we need to become preactive … Being proactive is agile; being preactive is being anticipatory" [118]

If you are only now becoming Agile, you are already too late because you are still reacting or pro-acting instead of preacting. We need to be predictably pre-active in a reactive world and to get there at a sustainable pace. All of this is possible with Flow, the UVF, and concepts like flash foresight. It is a clean simplification of all that is required to achieve exponential, "Nehemiah Effect" results.

Now go forth and do as much as is humanly impossible.

Appendix A

Flow Mini-case Studies

The best way to demonstrate Flow leadership is to use "Flow" using the I, We It and Its four-box along with the Vision Flow checklist. The following are a series of mini-case studies starting from the 1970's:

1. Farm Family Life
2. Steelcase InTandem SFA project
3. Steelcase Line 1 CRM project
4. Steelcase SDP project
5. InteliTouch
6. edgecom (merged later with Ericsson Business Consulting)
7. DNA Finland
8. PMI-Western Michigan (Project Management Institute)
9. Fruugo
10. Nature Publishing Group
11. OnStar / Global Connected Consumer, GM
12. The next example is yours!

We would also like to emphasize that these results are not ours alone. Teams Delivered each and every one of the following examples in these mini-case studies; and, almost all of the teams had been explicitly trained in the UVF and Flow.

The principles and tools we use for Flow and the Unified Vision Framework were key to the success of each and every assignment along the way. Without those, our teams would not have achieved the remarkable results that were Delivered. It was a collective effort and achievement.

1. Mini-case: Farm Family Life
(Value-add: USD $5.0 Million / Industry: Insurance and Finance)

This is one of the earliest realizations of the power of Flow to transform an organization. This case study hails back to the late 1970's and is a solid example of how the Unified Vision Framework was successfully implemented with a sales team. Ted was 27 years old when he moved to Cape Cod, Massachusetts to accept the position as agency manager for a small insurance agency that serves farmers in Eastern Massachusetts. The office he walked into was almost dead last in every metric used to determine success in the Insurance industry. The total premium generated by the existing staff of 13 people was $690,000 per year. In a healthy agency, one strong agent alone should be able to produce at that level. However, over the next four years, sales volume increased to over $5 million per year. The office had previously been losing US$41,400 per year (caused by a combined loss ratio of 1.06 for those familiar with Insurance metrics). By the last year of Ted's involvement profitability had increased to over $2 million per year.

This was accomplished by hiring, training and motivating a sales organization using the early-stage model of the framework, including the 1L + 1M + 1P = 1V formula (One Language + One Mind + One Plan = a Unified Vision). Later, we visualized this formula with the inverted triangle with the **Vision** in the middle:

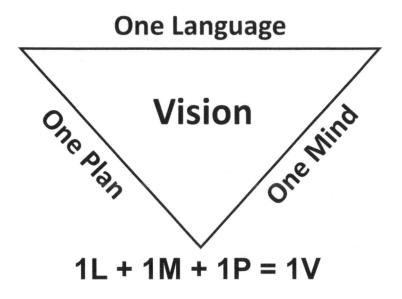

One Language

Vision

One Plan

One Mind

1L + 1M + 1P = 1V

This 1L + 1M + 1P = 1V formula actually mirrors the Flow formula for success:

Vision + Right People + the 4D Model = Successful Organization

This is because clear Definitions (1L) were agreed to (1M) and the plan (1P) was Distilled into simple action steps. It was an iterative, consistent and continuous process of applying this early iteration of the 4D Model (and the "one thing" of clear Vision) which created a successful organization.

What is great about this example is that it is completely outside of IT and demonstrates that Flow works really well in the Insurance industry. This was one of the original "Aha!" moments that grew into what we now call "Flow."

Since then, when we encounter an organization that is not as successful as they would like to be; and they have engaged our services, we use the root cause chart as a checklist to help us determine the key items that need to be changed in order to be able to Deliver Flow and its resulting success:

FARM FAMILY WAS EXPERIENCING THE FOLLOWING "UNDESIRABLE RESULTS (SEE THE "ROOT CAUSE CHART" IMAGE FOR THIS ON PAGE 82):"

Anarchy
x Anxiety
x Confusion
x Politics
Chaos
x Division

Achieving a spectacular 700% growth in four years and increasing sales to over $5 million per year; and, turning profitability from minus to plus, was a stunning organizational turnaround for this agency. It was achieved by applying the principles of Flow (in its earliest iteration it was called "the Model"). Implementing Flow removed the obstacles and blockers to success within the team as well as within the organization.

Using the "I, We, It and It's" four-box (that we shared earlier), the high-level picture of this successful turnaround looked like this:

I - PEOPLE

Used the "Model" to help organize each person in his or her daily sales activities and work. Individual meetings focused on the mental, physical, social and spiritual aspects of the person.

WE - TEAM LEVEL

Team Goals were established and weekly meetings were held to maintain visibility and show progress.

IT - PRODUCT / PROGRAM

Identified existing products that could be easily introduced to the established customer base and used creative training and sales approaches on all other products. This sales turnaround achieved a 700% growth in four years.

> ### ITS - EXECUTIVE / PORTFOLIO
>
> Ted used "the Model" i.e. 1L + 1M + 1P = 1V at all four levels of I, We, It and Its to organize the office and team.

The results of using "The Model," as Flow was originally called, were impressive. So much so that in each successive assignment, we have tracked the value-add that Flow has created. This first case was a great start!

2. Mini-case: Steelcase InTandem SFA project

*(Value-add: USD **$29+ Million** / Industry: Furniture and Office Systems)*

This was the first project that we worked on together as consultants. And, we also worked with our brother Dan, a Steelcase employee, who was the IT project lead. At that time Steelcase was the largest furniture and office systems manufacturer in the world. As this book goes to press, Steelcase is still number one in contract furniture sales with over $3 Billion in annual revenue.

This is the project where the utilization of the triangle as a visual tool (originally used at the individual level) moved to the organizational level as an additional part of the Unified Vision Framework. Dave O'Brien, Bill Kinsman, Ted and Dan were constructing an article that they presented to CIO Magazine on the success of the InTandem SFA project. The article was subsequently published in CIO. Dan drew a triangle to show how he (technology expert), Dave (business expert) and Bill (communication expert) had worked so well together as a team.

In observing the triangle, Ted was struck by how similar this picture was to the individual triangle he had used for managing team members at Farm Family and other organizations. The business expert was equivalent to the mental aspect of a person. The technology corresponded to the physical aspect. And, the communications expert matched the social aspect. The only thing missing was the spiritual (at the center) aspect. So, Ted walked up to the white board, flipped the triangle upside-down; and, added "Spirit" to the center of the triangle (Dan's version of the triangle was blank in the middle):

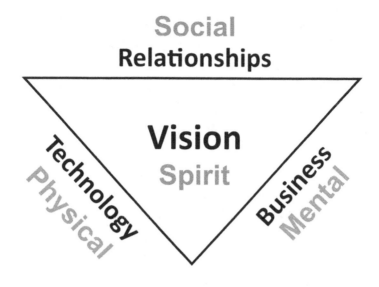

Spirit was later replaced with "Vision" at the center. We Define Vision at the center as a "Culture of Vision." This new organizational visual is core to implementing the UVF and Flow.

One of the key findings over the years is that there is almost universally a "disconnect" between the technology teams and the business teams on the two sides of the triangle above. And, this "disconnect" is due in large part to the fact that they actually speak two very different languages. There is a difference in the language used on the business side versus the technology side. There is also a disconnect between the language of teams and projects and executives. This is described above in Chapter 2 in the image that outlines the differences between the language of leadership versus the language of management.

The 1L + 1M + 1P version of the 4D Model was used for this project. Later, the four "D's" were Distilled into: Define, Distill, Deliver and Drive (see explanation in Chapter 2).

One of the first Definitions that we did was to re-craft the team's Vision statement down to a five to seven-word Distillation that was easy to remember, use and communicate. We used this as a team and as a communication vehicle to stakeholders as well. We did this by facilitating a Vision Definition and Distillation workshop with the team. It was also the first time that we incorporated the use of VSPT directly into a project, both at the individual and team level.

One of the top six consulting firms in the world had tried but had not been able to successfully implement the InTandem SFA (Sales Force Automation) system with the sales force and sales support teams.

Dan's team brought the project back in-house. In a very short period of time created an SFA system that worked. The book "Bold" explains why a small, internal team was able to significantly outperform top tier consulting group:

"With no bureaucracy, little to lose, and a passion to prove themselves, when it comes to innovation, small teams consistently outperform large organizations --- When you tell someone that they have only a tenth of the budget and tenth of the resources (or put conversely, you have to achieve 10x bigger results with the same resources-aka moonshot thinking), most people give up and say it can't be done. A few venturesome entrepreneurs may decide to give it a shot, but if they are paying attention, they'll understand from the outset that the same old way of solving the challenge will no longer work. The only option left to them is to throw out past experiences and preconditions and start with a clean sheet of paper. And this is exactly where serious innovation begins." [119]

PETER DIAMANDIS

And, this is exactly what Dan's team had done by the time we became involved in the project. We were called in to deliver the program to the sales and service organizations with a fresh perspective. During our initial assessment, this is what we found using the Vision Flow root cause table to now explain it:

THE STEELCASE (INTANDEM SFA) TEAM WAS EXPERIENCING THE FOLLOWING CHALLENGES:

Anarchy
x Anxiety
x Confusion
x Politics (*within the organization, not the team*)
Chaos
x Division (*within the organization, not the team*)

Dan's team was tasked with rewriting the software while Dave's team worked on rewriting the business process. To succeed the project also needed buy-in from a very skeptical sales organization. Ted was tasked with delivering the revised software to the sales force. Andrew worked with Dan who was the IT team leader in charge of all of the developers (the Technology side of the triangle) as well as the support team (over on the business side of the triangle). Ted also worked with Dave O'Brien, who owned the business side of the organization (the business side of the triangle) and Bill Kinsman (the communications side of the triangle) as a management consultant and subject matter expert in sales.

With Dan's help, we also worked with Bill Kinsman on training, internal marketing and organizational support (the Communications side at the top of the triangle). This contributed to a 70% conversion rate of the sales organization who began utilizing the SFA tool during their normal, everyday sales activities (this 70% rate of adoption was achieved during the first year after launch).

It is interesting that we were basically using all of the successful elements of Agile / Scrum almost a decade before Agile or Scrum had become formalized as frameworks or methodologies:

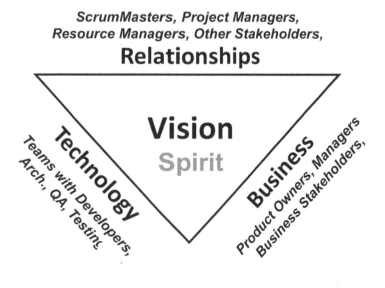

**ScrumMasters, Project Managers,
Resource Managers, Other Stakeholders,**

Relationships

Vision

Spirit

Technology
Teams with Developers,
Arch., QA, Testing

Business
Product Owners, Managers,
Business Stakeholders,

To make a very long story short, we successfully implemented the InTandem SFA suite of tools with the sales force and sales support teams using the UVF. We helped recover a failed project that no one, not the Executives or even the CEO, thought could be saved.

Steelcase's Director of Internal Auditing determined that the project's cost savings was over US$ 29 million net/net profit to the bottom line during the first 12 months after the successful launch.

Using the "I, We, It and It's" four-box, the InTandem SFA success looked like this:

I - PEOPLE

Using the UVF, we trained the project team members on how to improve and accelerate their daily work.

WE - TEAM LEVEL

Took a failed project and helped the team turn the project around and Deliver it successfully.

Facilitated the creation of the project Vision.

IT - PRODUCT / PROGRAM

Achieved an unprecedented 70% conversion rate for the sales force team members using the InTandem tool (over 400 sales people) along with 100% of the sales support teams (over 70 people). This success is one of the key reasons that CIO Magazine published the submitted article.

ITS - EXECUTIVE / PORTFOLIO

Used the UVF to communicate with stakeholders and Executives at all four levels of I, We, It and Its. This was also one of the first projects where we used Cascading Vision and VSPT at the team and individual levels.

In conducting a debriefing of the project's success (one of our first retrospectives), it became clear to us that we had just Distilled the "Model" into a framework for leading projects and organizations that could be easily replicated and repeated.

CIO Magazine published the article on the success of the InTandem SFA project, in part, because of the fact that up to that time no organization that they were aware of had been able to convert such a high percentage of technology-adverse sales people into avid users of an SFA tool.

3. Mini-case: Steelcase Line 1 CRM project
*(Value-add: **unknown** / Industry: Furniture and Office Systems)*

Excluding SingTel, this is possibly one of the most chaotic, fractured projects we've ever witnessed during the past 2 decades. All six "red flags" were flapping in the gale force winds of the existing organizational storm:

> ***USING THE VISION FLOW ROOT CAUSE TABLE, THE STEELCASE LINE 1 CRM PROJECT HAD THE FOLLOWING CHALLENGES:***
> x Anarchy
> x Anxiety
> x Confusion
> x Politics
> x Chaos
> x Division

One of our good friends, Brian Farish, asked the project leader to meet with Ted. Brian is a data architect and one of the top data modelers in the world. He was working with the technical team on the Line1 project and was observing and experiencing the severe project swirl that was occurring.

The project leader agreed to a meeting.

Ted used the newly formed organization triangle, Cascading VSPT and the 1L + 1M + 1P models to reveal and describe the "disconnects" and pain points in the project. After a couple of hours, the project lead had only one thing to say: "can you start tomorrow?" The answer was no, but soon thereafter Ted was serving fulltime as the external project lead helping re-orient and reorganize the project.

The project team was mostly co-located in a very old, run-down near windowless building on the Steelcase campus (it is now a parking lot). Working in this old, piece-of-junk building was a blessing because there were very few "fly-by" interruptions. Nobody just happened to go there, so it was a protected, strong and focused teaming environment. Since the building was mostly empty, there were many vacant rooms around the team area. A large 20-foot by 40-foot bunker abutted the team area. It was partially filled with old, mismatched furniture and had drab, off-white walls without windows. But, being so close, it was perfect for a team war-room, so we "acquired" it. We made the room the visible center of the Line1 universe. The team leader and Ted did their planning and brainstorming there. They also held the weekly team meetings in that space.

The project was very close to being shut down by senior management at Steelcase and there was a stakeholder update (a go/no go meeting) scheduled for around two weeks after Ted started. Ted used the bunker as the visual communication tool for that meeting.

Since the project had no Vision or Mission statement as a project and had not linked itself to the Steelcase Vision or strategic initiatives, that was the first thing that he did.

As we shared in the main part of this book, the line between the VS and PT represents the disconnect that exists in almost every organization between their Vision and Strategy(s) and the People and Tasks. This project was a classic example of a massive "disconnect" and its negative consequences. Using the war-room, they successfully linked the Steelcase Vision to the newly crafted project Vision and ultimately to the "Vision" for each team member as well (see the Cascading Vision image in the beginning of chapter 2).

The CIO article was used as a part of that communication link since the CEO and other executives had seen the article and were quoted in it. Alongside the CIO article, we included quotes by Steelcase executives from other business newspapers and periodicals regarding the importance of customer service.

In preparing the room for the executive meeting, the first thing Ted did was to print out the Steelcase Vision statement and also a copy of the 11 strategic initiatives for that current year. He then took a piece of yarn and taped it from the one strategic initiative that most closely fit the Line1 project and connected it to the project Vision statement.

Ted used large, desktop monthly calendars to create a big and visible timeline around the top of the room that showed all of the milestones and major activities that needed to be completed in order to successfully launch Line1.

At the stakeholder meeting, he quickly walked the Executives through the war room in a 10-minute demonstration of the project's Vision, strategies and status. At the end of the meeting, one of the executives turned to the CEO and said, "this is the best organized project in the history of Steelcase." This was actually not a true assessment since a tremendous amount of work still remained to be done. However, the link to Vision and the highly visible communications structure conveyed Line1's game plan effectively to the executives in their language. This big and visible link to Vision is a practice we have continued on all of our projects from that point forward.

As you can see, Vision was non-existent when Ted engaged with this project. The anarchy, anxiety, confusion, politics, chaos and division being felt by Mr. Farish reflected the presence of Flow anti-patterns and lack of the Flow elements necessary to succeed. All of the disconnects were addressed and brought into proper balance and Flow in a very short period of time. A seasoned coach will always be able to accelerate time frames with the proper support and level of authority.

Here are some of the highlights of what we were able to accomplish during the time we were there:

I - PEOPLE

Using the UVF, we trained the Line1 project leader and the team on how to improve and accelerate their daily work.

WE - TEAM LEVEL

Facilitated the creation of the project Vision and, for the first time, linked it to the overall Vision of the company. We did the hard work necessary to Define the elements needed by the project and project team. We then Distilled agreement between the appropriate stakeholders and re-worked the new plan based upon the agreed-to Definitions.

IT - PRODUCT / PROGRAM

We also created and used the "war room" as a big and visible communication tool for the team and to initially communicate with the Executives the status and future Delivery expectations for the project. It was also used daily by the team leadership and weekly by the team to maintain focus and momentum. We also used the room to on-board new team members so that they could quickly understand where the project was headed and where they fit.

ITS - EXECUTIVE / PORTFOLIO

We used "the Unified Vision Framework" in its earliest Distilled form, after the InTandem success, and we used it at all four levels of I, We, It and Its with remarkable results.

Unfortunately, this is one of the two case studies in this book where the politics reemerged so powerfully that the UVF was not able to successfully overcome the blocker. A little over six months into our involvement with this project, the Executive sponsor told us that he wanted a "soft launch" of the project six months early!

His Definition of a "soft launch" was to take the entire system and utilize it for one "small" product line. The problem with this idea was that the exact same number of dealers and organizational hand-offs and touch points needed to be in place whether you Delivered one product or the entire portfolio of products.

The reality was that a "soft launch" of this type was actually a full launch of the software. All of the software, systems and integrations necessary for a successful full launch simply could not be physically completed and tested six months early.

It just was not possible.

We spent the next two months using every tool, trick and management consulting method in our arsenal to try and convince him that this was not humanly, physically or technically possible. Being impossible, apparently, was not an impediment. As one person on the team put it (referring to the executive leadership), "unencumbered by knowledge, they moved forward."

The "soft launch" went forward and was an utter failure.

No framework, no matter how good, can counter balance the impacts of inappropriate decisions made at the leadership level. This case study, along with the Fruugo case below, are two examples that we have included in Flow where the UVF was unable to hold the original project timeframes against an organizational trajectory that had been altered by executive fiat.

4. Mini-case: Steelcase SDP project
*(Value-add: USD **$12 Million** / Industry: Furniture and Office Systems)*

This was a case where we worked together with the President of the Steelcase Design Partnership companies (a division of Steelcase at that time) to Define the concept, Deliver the development and implement a 30-60-90-day sales forecasting tool using the VSPT and 4D Models.

This was a relatively straightforward statement of work with a division within Steelcase that had a relatively clean and crisp Vision statement; but, there were still a few items on which to improve:

> ### USING THE VISION FLOW ROOT CAUSE TABLE, THE STEELCASE DESIGN PARTNERSHIP COMPANIES WERE EXPERIENCING THE FOLLOWING:
> Anarchy
> **x Anxiety**
> **x Confusion**
> Politics
> Chaos
> Division

This project was completed in a sixty-day time frame and it contributed to the division's 50% increase in sales (est. US$ 12 million) in the first year after implementation of the forecasting tool. Once again, the clarity and simplicity of the tool resulted in the majority of SDP sales people using it.

Using the I, We, It and It's four-box, the SDP success looked like this:

I - PEOPLE
Worked with the Executive and sales team leaders to Define and Distill the requirements for the forecasting tool.

WE - TEAM LEVEL
The sales teams fully converted to using the tool that they helped Define.

IT - PRODUCT / PROGRAM
This forecasting tool helped increase the SDP division's sales by 50% in the first 12 months after launch, creating an estimated increase of top-line revenue of US$ 12 million.

ITS - EXECUTIVE / PORTFOLIO
Used the Unified Vision Framework in one of its earliest forms with the SDP Executives and sales team leaders.

In retrospect, we probably should have used the billing model from Ted's dream (that we shared in the introduction at the beginning of this book) for this assignment. $780,000 per day would have been a much better reward structure (large smile emoji inserted here).

5. Mini-case: InteliTouch
(Value-add: USD $20.2 Million / Software Industry: Real Estate)

Ted was the primary UVF / Flow professional on this assignment. He was brought in by InteliTouch to help this dot com start-up do a turn-around.

The engagement was initiated after a one-hour conversation with the CEO, Steve Deckrow, in which Ted laid out the UVF and how it could be utilized within InteliTouch. The company hired Ted as a consultant to do an assessment and recommendation. Based on the recommendations, they offered Ted the role of Chief Operating Officer, which he accepted.

This was another assignment where all six areas were also up in flames:

THE INTELITOUCH PROJECT MANIFESTED THE FOLLOWING ISSUES:

- x Anarchy
- x Anxiety
- x Confusion
- x Politics
- x Chaos
- x Division

Even though Steve Deckrow had assembled a strong team and created a good corporate environment, they were still experiencing anarchy. Small tribes were trying to do the Right Thing, but without a unity of Purpose or a clear Vision. So, one of the first things Ted did in his new role was to refine and post the Purpose, Mission and Vision statements of the company everywhere in the office. He made it big and visible. He then trained all of the Executive team and much of the staff in the UVF.

Anxiety was also high when he began his engagement. Cash was flying out the door and collected revenue was low. InteliTouch was launched during the great dot bomb crash that happened globally. As the situation continued to spiral downward, the company cut its headcount from 140 to 39.

Clear Definitions were needed across almost all organizational and functional areas. Much of Ted's work focused on identification and correction of process and Definition problems. Some of these changes and results were:

- ☐ Cut the burn rate from $1.7 million to $350,000 per month, a savings of $1.35 million per month and $16.2 million per year
- ☐ Constructed a technical SWAT team that created a billing program that, in 30 days, increased collected revenue from $35,000 per month to $300,000 per month

- o This increased revenue from $420,000 per year to $3.6 million per year.
- o The new Billing structure and process improved the Collection Rate on Credit Card transactions from 35% (with >60% error rate) to 96% (with <1.5% error rate) and this dropped the Bank Fee for processing charges from 7% to 1.5% per transaction
- ☐ Reduced the elapsed time from "order placement" to "billable customer" from 38 days to 5.3 days in a 30-day period
- ☐ Ted assessed and recommended a change that reduced the monthly web hosting costs from $55,000 to $3,000, with no loss in service level or functionality (a savings of $52,000 per month; or, annual savings of $624,000)
- ☐ Identified the process and people required to bring all web design and customer service in-house, and by doing that it resulted in a US$ 250,000 per year savings
- ☐ In total, all of these corrective actions saved over USD $17 million per year in costs.

Using the I, We, It and It's four-box, the InteliTouch success looked like this:

I - PEOPLE

Trained staff on how to use the UVF in his or her daily activities and work. Unfortunately, had to reduce headcount from 140 to 39. However, many of the people who were let go still remain in contact and have a positive relationship with Ted to this day.

WE - TEAM LEVEL

Helped focus the teams on the highest, value-adding activities as Defined and filtered through the lens of Vision.

IT - PRODUCT / PROGRAM

Significant reductions in cost and increase in revenue while maintaining full functionality and exceptional customer service, as shared above.

ITS - EXECUTIVE / PORTFOLIO
Used the UVF to refine and keep visible the Purpose, Mission and Vision of InteliTouch at every level.

Still, after all of the changes listed above, the company was still losing USD $50,000 per month, so the investors chose to release Ted and the CEO. This action balanced the revenues and expenses so that the company was break-even. Ted's role at the end of this assignment was President and COO.

6. Mini-case: edgecom
(Value-add: USD $7 Million / Industry: Management Consulting for Telecoms, Finance, Banking)

This is one of the first times that Andrew used VSPT and the UVF outside of the Steelcase assignments. He was recruited and brought onboard at edgecom, a management-consulting firm, to lead the CRM and Program Management practices. edgecom was the management consulting division of Ericsson for the mobile telecom industry and was the first company in the world to license the VSPT Model (the name for the UVF and Flow at that time). DNA Finland, another licensee, followed soon after edgecom. One of Andrew's first edgecom assignments was SingTel (which is shared throughout the main body of this book).

The initial analysis of edgecom quickly revealed that the main area in which they needed to improve was with the overall organizational Vision:

EDGECOM HAD THE FOLLOWING CONCERN WHEN ANDREW JOINED THE ORGANIZATION:
x Anarchy
Anxiety
Confusion
Politics
Chaos
Division

Three years later, however, politics, confusion and anxiety crept into edgecom and it was eventually merged into the Ericsson Business Consulting division. edgecom had lost the internal political battle.

The I, We, It and Its for edgecom looked like this:

I - PEOPLE

Andrew and Ted trained close to 40 of edgecom's management consultants in the VSPT Model and the UVF (Unified Vision Framework). They were also trained on how to use it with the customers to increase satisfaction and, more importantly, to upsell additional services. The results were impressive to edgecom's leadership since, during fiscal year 2000, the teams increased edgecom's sales by over US$ 2 million above their projected revenue. This increase accounted for 1/7th of all annual sales revenues for edgecom during FY 2000.

WE - TEAM LEVEL

Andrew and Ted trained, coached and mentored edgecom's management consulting teams working on the DNA project as well as edgecom's teams at the headquarters in Stockholm. These teams were successful using the VSPT Model (UVF / Flow) at a number of customers, including SingTel, the launch of DNA Finland (see next Mini-case Study), etc.

IT - PRODUCT / PROGRAM

Andrew profitably led the PMO and CRM practices for edgecom, increasing top-line revenue by almost USD $7 million during the three years he was with edgecom.

ITS - EXECUTIVE / PORTFOLIO

edgecom grew from 40 consultants to 120 consultants from 1999 through 2002 while at the same time maintaining profitability

> throughout this 200% growth in size. edgecom was so pleased with
> this result that it licensed the VSPT Model (the UVF).

What was most amazing about the growth of edgecom between 1999 and 2002 is that it was able to triple in size while at the same time maintaining profitability (this was during the time that the first dot com bubble burst). This speaks directly to the power Flow Delivers to an organization, even during difficult economic times.

It is also a stellar example of being punished for your success. Great numbers and profitability were not sufficient to overcome the internal political battles.

7. Mini-case: DNA Finland
(Value-add: USD $29 Million / Industry: Telecoms)

This is another example of how the UVF was implemented throughout an entire organization (not just IT), top to bottom and from bottom to top and in ALL divisions of the organization: Sales, Marketing, Accounting, Legal, Operations, Networks, IT, etc. And, as in some of the other examples, all six flags were at full mast at the start even though it was a start-up:

> **THE DNA FINLAND PROJECT EXHIBITED ALL OF THE FOLLOWING:**
> x Anarchy
> x Anxiety
> x Confusion
> x Politics
> x Chaos
> x Division

Andrew arrived as the lead consultant with two other team members for a 90-day assignment to do an assessment and give recommendations for what needed to be done in order to launch DNA Finland on-time, on-budget and within scope.

Ted joined this project as a CRM specialist, but was quickly transitioned by the CEO to a role coaching the Executive leadership team. The CEO also appointed Andrew as the Interim COO and placed the IT Department, the Billing and Customer Care (CRM) team and the PMO under his direction. Ted and Andrew trained the entire Executive leadership team on how to use the VSPT Model (UVF / Flow) in each of their respective areas.

As with all of the other case studies, we always approach our engagements from a holistic, Vision-centric view:

I - PEOPLE

This was the first assignment that we used all of the tools that are included in the UVF and Flow: the VSPT Model, 1L + 1M + 1P = 1V, the 4D and 4R Models, Unified Vision, Cascading Vision and the concept of Flow. Not only were these tools all used at the individual level, but in all of the other 3 boxes (We, It and Its) as well.

WE - TEAM LEVEL

In addition to the Executive leadership team, over 250 of DNA's IT, CRM, PMO and Marketing team members were trained in the UVF and how to use it to Deliver "Wow!" results.

IT - PRODUCT / PROGRAM

Once again, we witnessed the ability of the UVF to handle an asynchronous organizational structure and Deliver laser-focused results to the key stakeholders, both internally and externally.

Similar to the Steelcase CRM case study above, we also used a war room at DNA. We created a portfolio view on the walls that we later called "the beast." This is because it listed all of the key projects and programs from floor to ceiling and wrapped around 3 walls of a relatively large conference room. This big and visible room was a powerful, highly visual communications tool.

ITS - EXECUTIVE / PORTFOLIO

Some of the best feedback that the UVF has ever received was from one of the team members that remarked that they "had never seen an Executive leadership team that was as unified as the one we had at DNA Finland." That is the essence of Flow, the UVF and the "one thing."

Two years and 16 additional edgecom team members later, DNA was not only launched, but it achieved a number of firsts in the world of mobile telecom operators:

- ☐ Having used VSPT and the UVF to simplify and refine the Vision, the executive management team also narrowed the marketing plan.
  - o This laser focus enabled the marketing team to successfully launch in 2001 and capture 5+% of the market in the first 11 months of operation and 16% within the first 2.5 years.
  - o What is extraordinary about this achievement is that no other mobile operator, that had entered any market worldwide as the fourth operator, had ever captured more than 7% of the market, regardless of how long they had been in business.
  - o Even more noteworthy is that this "out-of-the-park-home-run" was achieved in the most densely saturated mobile phone market in the world at that time: Finland.
- ☐ One of the most brilliant solutions that the UVF-trained teams Delivered was the idea of providing unlimited talk, text and a set amount of surfing to its customers (DNA was one of the first companies in the world to offer this type of mobile product).
  - o This reason they had to do this was that DNA did not have a functioning billing and customer care system that would be ready for use when the launch. So, they launched DNA Finland without a telecom billing system.

o However, the combined "flat-rate" product was an overwhelming success. In fact, they could not keep up with how fast the new subscriptions poured in.

The result --- sales and revenue dramatically increased for DNA. By the end of 2003 sales were €36 million per month. But, if they had only captured 7% of the Finnish market, as originally projected, then their sales would have been around €16 million per month. It could be argued that the additional value-add of having used the VSPT Model and the UVF was in the neighborhood of €20 million per month. In addition, the teams had also found the following savings opportunities:

☐ The IT department Delivered savings of more than US$ 4 million for fiscal year 2001, without reducing Deliverables or sacrificing quality of service.
☐ The IT team also negotiated an agreement structure with a Billing and Customer Care vendor that created an additional US$ 3 million in savings.

DNA is a great case study that mirrors the stunning successes achieved at both SingTel and Steelcase. Flow is repeatable not only across industries and cultures, but also across departments and divisions within an entire organization.

8. Mini-case: Successful use of the UVF and Flow with the PMI-Western Michigan Chapter (WMPMI, Project Management Institute)

(Value-add: USD $100,000+ / Industry: Volunteer Association)

Volunteer organizations provide an interesting challenge to the effective use and Delivery of any management system. If the system is not simple, it will not be followed. And, if it does not link to personal value and Vision, engagement fades and volunteers become a scarce commodity.

So, can applying the principles and framework elements of the UVF and Flow help with these issues? Yes. This case study unpacks how Ted applied Flow in his various roles as a volunteer leader for the Western Michigan Chapter of PMI.

First a little back story for why Ted became involved in WMPMI. Ted joined PMI and WMPMI in March of 2010 and became a certified PMP in June of 2010. Andrew had previously become PMP certified in 2006 while working at Nokia. After a stint at Fruugo (see case study number 9 below), Andrew had been applying the UVF and Flow in leading PMP Certification Test preparation boot camps for IIL (International Institute for Learning) across Europe, the Middle East and Africa. We also formed a relationship with Centria University in Kokkola, Finland to Deliver our own version of the PMP training based on Flow and the UVF. The first training sessions were conducted in Michigan by us in early 2010.

Since Ted was now involved in educating people on how to prepare to successfully pass a very difficult PMP Certification exam, he offered to join the education council for WMPMI. The council had been formed a year earlier and consisted of WMPMI Board members and representatives from local colleges and PMI registered education providers (REPs).

Ted's second meeting on this committee was in October of 2010. The council was brainstorming ways to improve relationships between businesses, academia and WMPMI.

Many ideas were brought up.

Ted suggested that WMPMI initiate a project management competition between student teams at local colleges and universities. After a robust and positive discussion, Kelly Talsma, the Vice President of Education for WMPMI, asked who would be willing to lead this effort. After an extended, uncomfortable period of silence with no one stepping forward, Ted offered to initiate the project with the understanding that he would probably not be able to follow through to completion due to a potential European engagement that was being finalized. This engagement for Ted didn't materialize when the CIO for the hiring company was fired, thus ending the engagement.

As a result, Ted remained project lead for the initiative. He and Kelly Talsma directed and successfully Delivered the implementation of "THE Project 2012 Intercollegiate Project Management Competition." The ramp-up to the January through April 2012 competition was crafted and executed during an 18-month period that began in October of 2010.

SINCE THIS WAS A START-UP, THERE WERE NONE OF THE FOLLOWING HAPPENING:

Anarchy

Anxiety

Confusion

Politics

Chaos

Division

Ted's first step as Project lead was to create the Vision, Mission and Purpose statements for the competition. He then iteratively led the steering committee through the 4D Model on a monthly basis during the run-up to the operational phase of the project's execution.

Ted and Kelly formed the leadership team that clearly Defined all the necessary Delivery aspects for the initial competition. This included a stellar panel of executive judges who agreed to evaluate the results achieved by each team, and, ultimately determine which four teams would share the cash prizes.

Because no competition of this type had ever been successfully accomplished by any PMI Chapter, anywhere in the world, there was no template that could be followed. So, much of the structure was developed on-the-fly, in a highly Agile way of working, using the Unified Vision Framework and Flow.

Also, since this was all new territory, continuous Distillation of Agreement between the relevant stakeholders was imperative. Ted and Kelly divided these responsibilities between themselves and, when needed, the steering committee.

The planning phase required intense recruitment of schools and a champion at each school along with a PMP Certified mentor for each team. Additionally, PMO panelists were needed to score and judge the project plans prior to the final competition day. Again, with no template from which to work, planning was done iteratively and adjustments and adaptations were made on a regular basis.

Finally, the event was successfully Delivered with seven teams from five schools participating.

The long-term Vision for THE Project was to make this an annual competition. The overwhelming success of the first competition laid the positive groundwork and has Driven the success forward during the ensuing years. As this book is going to press, THE Project will be completing its seventh year.

There were many positive impacts that resulted for WMPMI:

☐ Chapter visibility increased in almost every college and university in the WMPMI region

☐ The visibility of project management as a profession increased with some of the schools now including THE Project as part of their curriculum requirements for the students

☐ Increased visibility in the business community, enhanced by the partnership with the Grand Rapids Business Journal and other prominent community leaders

☐ The involvement of Millennials and Students in the WMPMI Chapter increased

☐ Corporate sponsorships for the Chapter increased from $ 1,500 in 2011 to over $ 100,000 in 2016:

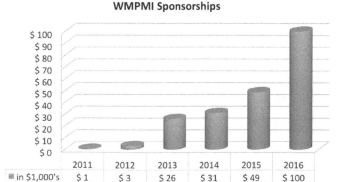

Total Raised 2012 – 2015 = $108,000+

WMPMI Sponsorships

	2011	2012	2013	2014	2015	2016
in $1,000's	$ 1	$ 3	$ 26	$ 31	$ 49	$ 100

THE Project has gained international recognition within the PMI community with a video regarding the 2012 competition being shown at the PMI Leadership Institute Meeting (LIM for EMEA) in May of 2012. Ted also presented at the PMI LIM (North America) in October of 2012 regarding the competition. At the October of 2015 LIM North America in Phoenix, Ted presented how the UVF and Flow increased sponsorships. During the 2012 presentation, Ted shared the following:

I - PEOPLE

Using the currency of relationships, Ted and Kelly recruited the Right People for the project.

WE - TEAM LEVEL

The unique Vision and potential of the competition was so compelling that, counter to the usual type of project done in a volunteer organization, Ted and Kelly were able to assemble a top-notch core team of volunteers from the WMPMI Chapter and the greater community to Deliver the project.

IT - PRODUCT / PROGRAM

This same Vision also drew a strong group of volunteers and participants for the steering group for the project.

ITS - EXECUTIVE / PORTFOLIO

The executive committee of WMPMI voted in January of 2011 to authorize $40,000 as a budget for first year of the competition. This was done as a pure experiment not knowing if any revenue would result from increased corporate sponsorships. This was a very bold move by the leadership team of a small PMI Chapter. Even though the competition lost money in the first year, it has been revenue-neutral every year since. However, the financial impact of the competition and Flow on sponsorships, can be seen in the overall picture shared above.

Also, to gain credibility and visibility within the academic and business communities, Ted recruited a powerful, well-known group of executives for the judge's panel. This included the former Lieutenant Governor for the State of Michigan and the Executive Editor for the Grand Rapids Business Journal. This level of executive buy-in from the community was fundamental to attracting schools, students and sponsors. Having the involvement of these executives was profoundly important for the successful launch. It was similar to the path that Peter Diamandis took in launching the XPRIZE competition a few years back where he describes the technique:

"Recruiting such big names gave us a number of advantages. For starters, just getting through the gauntlet of their due diligence, meant getting the benefit of their thinking. Having the smartest folks on the planet pound on your vision can help turn dank coal into glittering diamonds. More important, when we finally did launch, these names drew a crowd." [120]

This is exactly what we experienced at WMPMI with our judges panel.

For those of you that work with non-profits, associations, NGOs (non-governmental organizations), churches or any other type of volunteer organization, we would highly recommend utilizing the UVF and Flow to achieve your Vision.

9. Mini-case: Fruugo
*(Value-add: **unknown** / Industry: ecommerce start-up)*

Fruugo is the other example where the UVF was not able to alter the organizational flight path. We have included case studies like these to highlight the fact that there are no silver bullets. Any framework you choose, to achieve Flow, is ultimately tied to the quality of each and every team member that is part of the enterprise. And, if the True Vision of the organization is fractured or misaligned, then the probability of success drops dramatically.

Andrew came in on the project after it has already been up and running for around one year. This assignment was a challenge from the start. When Andrew arrived, Fruugo only had four of the six red flags flying. However, by the end of this assignment, the Anarchy and Politics, that were not initially visible, rose up and killed any potential for success.

USING THE VISION FLOW CHECKLIST, HERE'S WHAT FRUUGO LOOKED LIKE AT THE START OF THIS ASSIGNMENT:

Anarchy
- x **Anxiety**
- x **Confusion**

Politics
- x **Chaos**
- x **Division**

The Anarchy that Fruugo experienced at the end of this assignment was there, but not visible, at the beginning. This was due to a lack of Distilled Agreement regarding what the Definition of Fruugo's True Vision was. The Board of Directors had one understanding, the Executive leadership team had another and the delivery teams had their own.

The Vision and culture of the company ended up being fractured. As a result, the entire organization suffered greatly. For an expanded discussion on fractured Vision see our section on the Four types of Vision in Chapter 4 of "The Nehemiah Effect" on pages 59 through 70.

Since half of Fruugo's employees were from a Traditional (Waterfall) background and the other half were Agilists trained in Scrum, this created a cultural clash at the team and individual level. They were experiencing a very high level of anxiety. And, this fractured culture was enough to continuously derail even good ideas.

The Agile purists were convinced that the teams that were using a Traditional approach would doom the organization to destruction. The Traditionalists felt the exact same way about the Agilists. There was no unity between the warring tribes and no unifying Vision to bring them together. This division was a key blocker to Fruugo's success. The creation and maintenance of unity is a key responsibility of senior leadership.

At Fruugo, that unity never occurred.

What is interesting about the Fruugo case is that this was one time where Andrew was able to put an Agile team side-by-side with a Traditional team on the same type of work assignment and compare the results. It probably wasn't a fair comparison, but the Traditional team outperformed the Agile team dramatically during a number of iterations (Fruugo was using a 2-week Sprint for its iterative cycles). This caused quite a bit of consternation for the Agilists. The best they could come up with was that the Traditional team was actually "Agile" since that team had been working together for years and the Agile team had never worked together before Fruugo. The Agilists had to begrudgingly admit that short-cycle waterfall, done by an experienced team was actually more effective (in this case) than Agile done by an inexperienced team.

There was also a high level of confusion between the teams since the Definitions between teams were not in alignment. Thus, integration and cross-dependencies were causing major problems. In fact, the releases were routinely so broken that the teams became very skilled at rolling back to previous versions of the platform to undo the damage the confusion caused.

The turf battles were fierce and resulted in an amazing level of politics for a start-up. The resulting chaos was at such a frenzied level that the CEO described the situation as the "wild west." But, both the CEO and Andrew thought the situation could be turned around, despite a mountain of evidence to the contrary.

The division at the team level was so deep back in 2008 that, in order to try to create unity, the CEO decided to send the team members from traditional and/or waterfall backgrounds to a Certified ScrumMaster (CSM) training course that was customized for Fruugo. Barely half of the team members came away from the CSM training willing to give Scrum (Agile) a fair try. Once again, this demonstrated an institutionalized lack of unity not addressed by the executive team. Training alone does not necessarily change imbedded cultural antibodies.

The PMO that Andrew led was Agile and able to Deliver unified reporting to the executive management team despite having to deal with both synchronous and asynchronous information in the reporting feeds from the teams. But, the trends and the forecasts that were communicated to the executive team were not accepted as accurate or valid by the leadership. But, in the end, the forecasts Delivered by Andrew ended up being spot-on accurate.

The cost of delay in bringing the final product to the market was, in this case, in excess of €40 million. And, the product that was originally envisioned and sold to investors never made it to market.

The power of the UVF drains away in toxic Cultures or where trust does not exist. The attempt to turn Fruugo around included the following:

"I" (INDIVIDUAL) WINDOW

Around 120 team members were trained in using the UVF as well as Scrum. However, training people that do not want to change will always be ineffective and will not Deliver the intended results. The antibodies will rise-up and kill off the new way of working.

"WE" (TEAM) WINDOW

Eventually, all teams used the UVF and Scrum to Deliver their work in two-week cycles, but not all were willing participants. Some went through the motions, but never really reached the "Aha!" moment described in Flow. This is a perfect example of challenges created by leadership disunity; and, confusion in Definitions and Distilled Agreements.

"IT" (PRODUCT / PMO) WINDOW

As the PMO Director, Andrew led the Waterfall to Agile Transformation for Fruugo. Sadly, by the time he joined the team, the damage created by the institutionalized disunity was so severe that this situation could not be rescued or turned around from the PMO level within the timeframe available.

"ITS" (ORGANIZATION) WINDOW

In retrospect (and hindsight is always more accurate that foresight), it was clear that the Waterfall-to-Agile transformation was initiated too late and too far down in the food chain to turn the ship around.

The burn-rate for Fruugo was well over €10 million per year and the final cost for this "experiment" ended up over €40 million. In fact, one of the headlines from Arctic Startup summed it up best: "Nearing Bankruptcy, Fruugo Burned Through €40 Million to Generate €100K" see:

http://arcticstartup.com/article/fruugo-financials-bankruptcy/

While Fruugo still exists today, it is doubtful that it has ever earned a profit. It was eventually merged with a bankrupt online retailer in the UK.

The original idea for Fruugo was actually a good one. For example, Fyndiq in Sweden is a mirror image of Fruugo, with the small exception that Fyndiq is making money. The main difference is that Fyndiq went to great lengths to learn from Fruugo's mistakes and made sure that they didn't repeat them.

One key difference between the two cases is that Fyndiq kept it small and succeeded in Sweden first, before opening up new markets in other parts of Europe. Fyndiq also has a more reasonable fee structure for the participating merchants, thus making it a more attractive platform for building additional sales for small merchants.

The major difference between the SingTel and Fruugo cases is that the Executive leadership at SingTel listened and adjusted accordingly. Fruugo is a classic case of pride going before destruction. It was a very expensive demonstration that a house divided cannot stand.

10. Mini-case: Nature Publishing Group
(Value-add: USD $18 Million / Industry: Publishing / Media)

This case study demonstrates how a clearly Defined Vision for change can be achieved with persistent, focused Delivery. It is a step-by-step process over a longer period of time. However, while most companies would have spent five to seven years to achieve this level of transformation success, NPG was able to achieve it in under two years, stunning their competitors.

When Andrew arrived at Nature Publishing Group (NPG) in January of 2011 his mandate as the Portfolio Manager consisted of leading the Waterfall-to-Agile transformation for NPG along with resurrecting the PMO (Program Management Office). He reported to both the Chief Technology Officer (CTO) and the Chief Operations Officer (COO).

NPG previously had a traditional PMO in 2006, but the individual leading that effort had been promoted and NPG had not back-filled the role. It took almost five years before the pain was at a high enough level for NPG to react and restart the PMO. This time around NPG wanted to take the opportunity to create an Agile PMO.

In 2010, NPG could Deliver, on the average, just under 60 medium-sized projects per year (medium-sized projects were Defined as the work that could be accomplished by a team in roughly four to six months' duration). However, the number of projects in the queue was over 250. This meant that NPG only had a 1-in-4 chance of doing the right project at the right time.

Using VSPT and the 4D Model (Define, Distill, Deliver and Drive), Andrew began the process of Defining the structure of the Agile PMO. This included projects, programs and portfolios; Agile tools, techniques and templates; and, Agile reporting. The PMO set a cadence of bi-weekly meetings with the project managers, ScrumMasters and Product Owners.

At the same time, using VSPT and the 4D Model, Andrew put together the Agile Transformation Group. This group functioned as the Agile Governance Group and consisted of stakeholders that reported to the Executive team. It had the primary responsibility of Defining and Distilling what later became known as "NPG Agile." This was the minimum viable Definition of what a team was required to do and still be considered "Agile."

Andrew worked with the Board of Directors to hone the Vision for each of their respective areas of responsibility. One of the first things he did was to divide the Portfolio into two parts:

- ☐ Science-for-Scientists
- ☐ Science-for-non-Scientists

By the way, for those of you that are not familiar with NPG, its flagship publication, "Nature Journal," is the top journal in the world in Science, Technology and Medicine (STM). And, a long list of Nobel laureates have been published in Nature. Nature, and the journals associated with Nature, is targeted at the STM community.

"Scientific American," also published by NPG, is targeted at those individuals with a deep interest in Science, but who may work in other professions. Historically NPG is known as a well-run, professional organization. However, this is what Andrew found upon his arrival:

FOUR OF THE SIX ANTI-PATTERNS WERE HAPPENING:
Anarchy
x Anxiety
Confusion
x Politics
x Chaos
x Division

To combat these anti-patterns, the Portfolios and departmental Visions were refined and NPG Agile Defined. After those were agreed-to by the newly-formed Agile Governance Group, then the real work on transforming Nature began. Using the transformation four box, the following were done in parallel:

I - PEOPLE

For the "I" (Individual) window, all 250 team members, from the CEO, CTO, COO, etc., level to the team level were trained in "NPG Agile" and the UVF (Flow). This was a drink-from-the-fire-hose half-day session. Of the over 250 team members trained at NPG, there were only two or three people that were overtly resistant to the idea of changing the way they worked (see "Aha!" image in Chapter 3).

When transitioning from Waterfall to Agile, every person struggles in the beginning with the "yes, but..." roller coaster ride. Eventually they go through the motions, but still aren't fully convinced that Agile and Flow work. There is a point during the transformation where the light bulb goes on and the person has what we call the "Aha!" moment where they understand that Agile and Flow do not just "work," but that they work very well.

From that point forward, they begin to perform and learn more-and-more through experience and experimentation. As enthusiasm and excitement grows, they find a way to move themselves into personal hyper-performance and do their utmost to take the team there as well.

The "Aha!" curve described in Chapter 3 applies to the team, product and organizational windows. A full-blown transformation at a large organization, without strong executive leadership utilizing Flow, can take five to seven years, or longer. This is because an individual transformation in an un-supportive culture can take up to two or three years. And, as we mentioned earlier, seasoned coaching can decrease this time frame.

WE - TEAM LEVEL

Andrew coached, trained and mentored the teams. The teams that were struggling implementing Agile required a high-level of "hands-on" attention to coach and mentor them up the transformation curve. A couple of the teams that were consistently not meeting expectations for the transition were trained a second time in "NPG Agile" as well as being sent to external courses led by external trainers to help them gain fresh perspective.

One interesting effect that Andrew observed was that it only took moving one or two teams from each of the clouds (see the Aha! Curve image in Chapter 3) to the next level up (towards the hyper-performing end of the curve) to achieve remarkable results and double the productivity of all the teams'.

IT - PRODUCT / PROGRAM

Getting the Product, Program and Project management under control in the "IT" (Product/Program) window represented one of the biggest challenges in the transformation. When Andrew arrived, the teams were discouraged by the mountain of work that needed to be completed in a very short period.

To help better lead the Portfolio and Program management, the projects were divided into 2 Portfolios: Science for Scientists (business-to-business) and "Science for non-Scientists" (business-to-customer). And the PMO created both the project and release road maps. A couple of the tools that were used included what we call the Walkabout Workshop and the Cutting Room Floor exercises.

The Walkabout Workshop is our version of "big-room" Portfolio planning. It consists of getting the Board members and their direct reports in a room and agreeing on which projects will be included in which portfolio. Once the projects were divided into 2 Portfolios, they were also sorted at the Program level into what became known as the "Quadrants" (a 4-box dashboard we used in the Agile PMO).

These Quadrants were included as part of the Cutting Room Floor exercise. NPG's project completion velocity meant that there was about 4.5 years' worth of work to Deliver in the Project Backlog. Worse, since every executive wanted and expected their projects to be Delivered in the next twelve months anyway, there was only a 1-in-4 chance that the right projects would be done during the next 12 months.

Andrew and the ATG helped the Board shift their focus from the entire Project Backlog to concentrating on the top 100 projects that would be Delivered during the next 15 months. 150 projects were "cut" from the list published to the teams. When the teams heard that 150 projects had just been cut, their hope was renewed. Suddenly, what had previously been viewed as unachievable quickly became a "stretch goal" that had a chance of success. Although this was a small and seemingly subtle change, the impact on team morale was enormous.

Many times, organizations misunderstand that during the first year of a transformation productivity often goes down by as much as 20%. So, we should have anticipated being able to Deliver only 48 projects in 2011 while going through the Waterfall-to-Agile transition. But, the teams at NPG Delivered 72 projects that first year (20% more than in 2010); and, they did it while they were in the middle of a Waterfall-to-Agile transformation.

That is a testament to the power of the UVF and Flow.

In 2012, the teams Delivered 98 projects and by mid-year 2013 they were on track to Deliver 124 projects for the year. It's not just that they doubled their output during that time, but we could assure the executive leadership that the highest priority projects were being Delivered first (thus going from one-in-four chances of Delivering the most valuable projects to well over 80% of the most valuable work items being Delivered at the right time).

Remember the original list of 250 projects? What would have taken four-and-a-half years to Deliver was Delivered in less than three years (72 + 98 + 124 = 294).

The standard cost for an Agile team of eight people is roughly USD $1 million per year. Using that figure to reverse engineer the value-add that Flow contributed to NPG, this was the same as saving budget dollars (team costs) of at least $18 million since we eliminated over one year off the original estimate of the time needed to Deliver the original project backlog.

This was achieved without adding any additional resources to the team. In fact, due to attrition, we had fewer team members in 2013 than 2011. This aligns with the "4 Whys" that we use at the Portfolio, Program and Project levels:

1. Increase Revenues
2. Decrease Costs
3. Eliminate / Mitigate Risks
4. Do the Right Thing

These are the key measures that should be included in the business case for doing a project, product, program, process or portfolio.

Its - Executive / Portfolio

The big room planning and cutting room floor exercises raised the odds of doing the right project from only 1-in-4 to around 8-in-10. By the end of 2013, the teams were on track to clearing the entire project backlog of the original 250 projects, over one year ahead of the original velocity.

One of the other tools used at the executive leadership level was a clarified and simplified functional Vision.

NPG's Vision/Mission statement was from 1868. It was over half a page long. If we were to lock the executives in a room, give them two minutes to have them write NPG's Mission statement down, word-for-word from memory, then they would fail. Except for people with photographic memories, it would be impossible for any of the executives remember it.

We routinely train Flow Professionals that an organizations' Vision, Mission, and Purpose statements need to be short (5 to 7 words). Those need to be memorable and easy to communicate.

The NPG Mission statement was neither of those.

As stated above we Distilled the functional Vision statements down to "Science-for-Scientists" and "Science-for-non-Scientists." These functional statements functioned rather nicely (7 words, total) for the PMO. Although the executives agreed that the Mission statement was too long --- and outdated --- not a lot of headway was made Distilling the half-page document to 5 to 7 words. Nevertheless, the Portfolio proxy "Vision" statements plugged the communications gap that existed between the executive leadership (and organizational legacy) and the rest of the organization.

Splitting the work into two portfolios saved the company millions of dollars (i.e. cost avoidance) since technology, infrastructure and operational support projects (that were trying to create synergies where none existed) were eliminated. The Executive's original thinking was that Scientific American (Science-for-non-Scientists) could be managed the same way as Nature Journal (Science-for-Scientists). That, however, was not the case since the anticipated cost savings from using the same systems, management, platforms and infrastructure never materialized due to operation differences.

Trying to create a common organizational leadership process and platform that could be used by both seemed like a good idea to leverage scarce resources. However, it was a less than optimal idea for either business. Once the Portfolio adjustments were made, the teams could focus on the projects that supported and added value to both Portfolios. By separating the Portfolios, the organization Delivered the value that each group desired.

What did the extra complexity that existed prior to Flow cost that company?

Our estimate is that this cost NPG roughly $18 million over a four-year period of time. Further, since NPG delayed going Agile by at least five years, the delay easily cost them an additional $23 million. This was not only painful for the organization, but very expensive.

The end of NPG's Agile journey is still being written.

Due to business decisions made in London, almost everything that had been achieved by the teams in NY and London was, more-or-less, dismantled due to an internal reorganization. The CTO for NPG in NY was made redundant. And, the new CTO who was hired in London came from a very traditional, command-and-control background. He and his new PMO leadership team decided to revert to Prince2.

Jeff Sutherland, co-founder of Scrum, related a similar experience:

"After I left PatientKeeper, a new management team decided Scrum wasn't the best way to run things anymore. The result? Product releases dropped from forty-five a year to two, revenue dropped from fifty million dollars a year to twenty-five, and attrition, which had been less than 10 percent, shot up to over 30 percent. They went from a great company back to mediocre performance by returning to traditional corporate behavior." [121]

In other words, what happened at NPG was a giant step backwards. Although the new CTO had promised that the NY teams would stay intact and that the technology teams would not be moved and centralized to London, that was a promise that was not kept.

Eventually a lion's share of Technology was moved to London.

And, although some form of Flow and "Agile" may still be in use in some areas at NPG, it is not clear from the outside as to whether they are enjoying the same project success or velocity (as they did when Andrew was coaching and mentoring NPG in its journey to Agile and Flow).

Andrew chose to move on. This was one of those cases where culture and politics ate everything for breakfast, lunch and dinner.

However, Macmillan's decisions in no way diminish the stunning successes achieved by the NPG teams as they transitioned from Waterfall to Agile and Flow. This case study demonstrates that the "Its" window can be one of the roughest and toughest areas to transform.

As of 2015, Macmillan and Springer merged forming Nature Springer. And Kent Anderson shared in the following analysis in a blog post:

"An interesting side note is that the CEO of Macmillan, Annette Thomas, will become the new organization's Chief Scientific Officer. Derk Haank of Springer

will be the new CEO of the combined entity; he is bringing his COO and CFO along, which suggests that the new entity will be focused primarily on financial and operational performance, which makes sense if they are grooming it for an IPO." [122]

Even with the full support of the Board of Directors and Executives, truly transforming to and sustaining a journey to a high-performing Flow and Agile culture can be a challenge, especially considering the dizzying speed at which enterprises routinely carry out re-organizations, mergers and acquisitions.

11. Mini-case: General Motors OnStar,
*(Value-add: estimated minimum USD $4 **Million** / Industry: Automotive)*

This case study is an example of Delivering value above and beyond what was included in the statement of work. Andrew was brought in initially to help coach the Executives at OnStar on how to become more Agile at the Enterprise level. Ted was added to the team as an additional Enterprise Agile Coach. During the assignment, we found that OnStar's project management and program management were a challenge to understand since most of the PMO and project management functions were decentralized, controlled, funded and led by multiple line management leaders.

The CIO had a small Portfolio management team that reported directly to him. The PMO reported to another executive. And, the ePMO (Enterprise Program Management Office) reported to still another executive in a different division of General Motors. Further complicating all of this was the fact that all project managers reported directly to the individual, functional line managers.

It was important to get agreement on the Definition of "the big picture" between the various silos and put it in place quickly. In other words, we started with clarifying the Vision from the top so that the teams and functional units would understand where they fit and what they were supposed to Deliver.

To solidify this agreement, we created a large, visible depiction of all key OnStar projects planned for 2014. These were put in a matrix on the wall in a conference room. This was the room in which most of our team was co-located. We took the longest wall (a floor to ceiling whiteboard) and created a "beast" portfolio view for all the key programs and projects expected to be Delivered during 2014. Most of the projects in the matrix were focused on the 2017 production cycle.

We brought in each of the line managers responsible for the projects and programs and walked them through the room. We then asked them, visually, if the facts were correct on the board (scope, time, budget and resources). This helped everyone understand when OnStar would run out of people and/or money for their projects. Without exception, the line managers barely made it a third of the way through their own projects before running out of either people and/or money. After interviewing all the line managers, we then visually drew a budget "waterline" running across the entire beast, although the list had not yet been prioritized.

We then brought in the executives and shared the results.

Their reactions were priceless.

Previously, no one had visually communicated to them the big picture across all silos. The executives then adjusted and prioritized based on the information captured in the beast. This was done in a 14-hour cage-fight that determined the 2014 road map based on the matrix. This resulted in cost avoidance that otherwise would have been missed, and agreement was reached.

USING THE CHECKLIST, ONSTAR HAD THE FOLLOWING ANTI-FLOW ISSUES WHEN WE ARRIVED:

x Anarchy

x Anxiety

x Confusion

x Politics

x Chaos

x Division

The executives loved the beast/wall and had the Portfolio team capture the entire beast into a spreadsheet from which they could continue to work in a distributed fashion. They never did seem to understand the power of maintaining the whole picture in such a big and visible format. Once we left the project, the beast was removed from the wall and the spreadsheet ruled.

Instituting Flow and visibility accelerated the process and reduced the average time to gather requirements from 18 to 3 months for the three teams we worked with directly. This led to a direct, estimated savings of USD $1,5 million per team. The combined value-add to OnStar was over USD $4 million. It also enabled some teams to complete their work early by an entire year based on previous schedules.

I - PEOPLE

Due to the nature of this assignment, neither Ted nor Andrew were tasked with any type of coaching, mentoring or training for the individual team members at OnStar. However, Ted conducted a lunch and learn webinar for Flow and the UVF for over 400 GM employees. There may have been personal benefits realized by individual employees utilizing the Flow and UVF in their daily work after the webinar.

WE - TEAM LEVEL

We worked with the leadership teams to create the big picture, gain agreement and to identify areas of potential savings for OnStar. These agreements were then implemented at the development team level.

IT - PRODUCT / PROGRAM

The "beast" big picture for the Portfolio view was used with the line management and executives to identify savings, gain agreement and to level-set expectations across the organization regarding what could be Delivered during the following year.

Scrum and Flow techniques were used to decrease the requirements gathering process from 18 months to 3 months (one team reduced it to one month). This gave OnStar the opportunity to move up the launch of many features by a full model year.

ITS - EXECUTIVE / PORTFOLIO

We created a war room with a large matrix to give OnStar an Agile and Flow Portfolio view that showed where the resources and money ran out. Being able to visually see the big picture as well as creating the opportunity for the executives to have frank and open discussions with line management about what could be accomplished was acknowledged as extremely valuable by the executive leadership team. Alignment had not been happening prior to our involvement. It required bringing in seasoned Enterprise Agile Coaches to facilitate this.

Our time at OnStar was short, but effective. And, this is one of those cases where we should have used the invoicing method that Ted shared in his dream at the beginning of this book.

12. Mini-case: Grand Rapids Community College PeopleSoft Financials and PeopleTools Upgrade

(Value-add: between <u>US $75,650 to $162,650</u> / Industry: <u>Higher Education</u>)

Grand Rapids Community College (GRCC), located in Grand Rapids, Michigan, has 29,000+ students from all walks of life enrolled in traditional liberal arts and occupational courses, adult education courses, and skilled training courses and apprenticeships. GRCC uses PeopleSoft as its enterprise resource planning (ERP) system to manage its records. It is also known at the college as "the system of record." The PeopleSoft modules that GRCC uses are Campus Solutions (enrollment, grading, student information, etc.), Human Resources (payroll, employee management and records, hiring and termination, etc.), and Financials (billing, campus accounting, purchasing, etc.). Every few years, each of these systems must be upgraded, which requires a great deal of time and effort from IT staff, various college departments, and outside consultants.

GRCC's IT Project Management Office received a project request in January 2016 to upgrade PeopleSoft Financials from version 9.1 to version 9.2, which included a PeopleTools upgrade. Work began on the project on July 26th, 2016. An ERP upgrade like this without fully dedicated consultants typically takes six to eight months to complete, depending on the skills, experience, and availability of the team. The last upgrade to GRCC's PeopleSoft Financials system took place from August through October 2012. This project was done by a paid, dedicated, expert consultant and took three months to complete at a cost of US $167,000. Given that GRCC possessed the right people to do the project at the time it was initiated, they decided to limit the consulting budget to US $55,000 and an additional US $25,000 for training for a total of US $80,000. They scheduled the go-live for February 13th – six months from the project start date – which was considered an optimistic estimate.

USING THE VISION FLOW ROOT CAUSE TABLE, GRCC'S PEOPLESOFT FINANCIALS AND PEOPLETOOLS UPGRADE PROJECT HAD THE FOLLOWING CHALLENGES:

Anarchy

Anxiety

x Confusion

x Politics

Chaos

Division

The project manager for the project, Jeff Kissinger, is a Flow Certified Professional and Flow Certified Trainer. He suggested to the project sponsor and the key stakeholders that they take an Agile approach to the project. Given that they've only known and practiced Traditional project management – complete with weekly status meetings and Microsoft Project Gantt Charts – they reluctantly agreed to try this.

Jeff first worked with the team to define the project vision: A well-running 9.2 PeopleSoft Financials system. Not necessarily a sexy vision, but it is seven words, memorable, and any team member knew it when asked, so it worked well. He also gathered the initial requirements for the project in one hour by facilitating a product roadmap discussion armed with sticky notes, markers, and a white board. The next day, he created a 3 x 3 Kanban board to facilitate the tracking of the sprint backlog, work in progress, and completed tasks / increments. This was placed next to a product board he created that contained all the requirements gathered in the product roadmap discussion (and subsequent sprint planning meetings), but were now color coded by epic, feature, and user story categories. Each were placed within their respective level of priority on the product board.

Jeff trained the core project team on the basics of Scrum in 30 minutes using "The Candy Game," – a technique he learned and taught in Flow certification classes with Ted and Andrew. This game breaks down the essentials of Scrum using nothing more than individually wrapped candy, a white board, a marker, and the team members. He then spent the next 30 minutes providing a simple overview of Flow and its principles and how it relates to the project. This information was referred to throughout the project life cycle whenever the project team encountered issues.

The greatest amount of confusion on this project, identified at the beginning, was between the IT Enterprise Applications Department and the IT Infrastructure Department. This centered on server development, provision, and availability, human resource allocation, and database refresh frequency. Jeff quickly identified these as the Flow Anti-patterns of confusion and politics and scheduled a meeting between the two departments to resolve these matters. This meeting, which lasted less than 30 minutes, focused on defining Infrastructure's requirements and expectations for this project. Once this was done, both parties agreed on the number of servers needed, the people needed, and when they will be needed at key points in the project. This eliminated the political issues between the two departments.

Typically, ERP upgrade projects at GRCC are very chaotic and stressful. They involve over 1200 tasks and steps sequenced in a specific order and are often repeated in a series of practice go-lives to ensure accuracy and proper timing. Troubleshooting issues is a big factor, too, which means any mistakes have a detrimental effect on the project's timing and team dynamics. Using Scrum and Flow to manage the project exposed all potential and actual issues very quickly, which allowed the team to quickly deal with them using Flow techniques. Any time a Flow Anti-pattern was identified, the team quickly went into solution mode to resolve it. This behavior became habit within the first month.

The team operated on two-week sprints. Each sprint review was quickly followed with a retrospective of the sprint, which always drew the team closer together and drove them and the project to a higher level of efficiency and effectiveness as they planned the next sprint. Within one month of using Flow and Scrum to manage this project, the team – at first reluctant – was fully engaged in the process. Tasks and issues most often missed or exaggerated in past ERP project upgrades were dealt with using a minimal amount of effort and time.

The upgraded system went live on December 5th, 2016 – 2 ½ months ahead of schedule. This was only two weeks longer than the dedicated, paid consultant took to do the last upgrade in 2012. What's more, only US $ 4,350 of the US $80,000 project budget was spent on consulting, which saved GRCC US $75,650 (no additional training was needed). Of course, if they would have used a dedicated consultant like they did in 2012, the savings is much more substantial at US $162,650.

Probably more impressive is the time savings. The team working on the project still had to perform its break/fix maintenance duties on the various systems they collectively maintain for GRCC outside the project throughout the project life cycle, which means they were not dedicated to the project 40 hours or more a week like the consultant. Also, the early go-live allowed the project team's resources to be reallocated to other projects 2 ½ months earlier than they had planned. This savings has had a major effect on the timing of these projects and the benefits they provide the IT department and college at large. As an extra added bonus, getting the project done before Christmas made for a more relaxing holiday season for the team.

Here are some of the highlights of what was accomplished:

I - PEOPLE

The individual project team members repeatedly said this project was the least stressful ERP upgrade they had ever experienced. Each of them had time to tend to their personal and professional responsibilities with little or no disruption.

WE - TEAM LEVEL

The team worked very well together. Although skeptical of the process at first, once they saw the value of the process, they became its champions and performed exceptionally well. They especially enjoyed the autonomy of being a self-managed team. Although the project is closed, the enterprise analysts who worked on the project kept the Kanban board in their area and use it religiously to manage their everyday work.

IT - PRODUCT / PROGRAM

The PeopleSoft 9.2 upgrade and the PeopleTools upgrade that preceded it was very successful. Not only did the upgrade go live 2 ½ months early, the project experienced minimal issues during the first week after go-live. Since then, it has performed exceptionally.

ITS - EXECUTIVE / PORTFOLIO

GRCC's Chief Information Officer, Jeff's boss, generously invested money and time into his training as a Flow Certified Professional and Flow Certified Trainer. He is very pleased with the results.

This case study is a great example of the power of Flow adding value in a non-profit organization. It also demonstrates that others can take the principles of Flow and achieve the same remarkable results in their own organizations (without having to have either Ted or Andrew shepherd them through the process).

13. Mini-case: Procare Commercial Landscape
(Value-add: US $550,000 / Industry: Landscaping Services)

Procare Commercial Landscape Services was profitable every year for 24 consecutive years. Dirk Bakhuyzen had worked his way up from hired hand to owner and had just experienced his first annual loss. Procare lost $250,000 which is a serious situation for a company with 2.5 million in top line revenue. Dirk's accountant, Doug Postma, had been going through a Flow transformation of his accounting firm and recommended that Dirk meet with Ted to discuss the situation. As a result of the meeting Dirk engaged Ted in a consulting role for ½ day per week for a year to help him turn the situation around.

The work was not exclusively "Flow" due to Ted's extensive experience as an Executive coach but everything discussed and implemented was initiated and completed through the lens of Flow:

- ☐ Honing the company Vision
- ☐ Clearly Defining core processes, tools and people
- ☐ Distilling Agreement with all relevant stakeholders for each change
- ☐ Planning in short cycles with weekly reviews that kept progress visible

As with all of the other 12 mini-case examples we've looked at so far, we begin with the Flow checklist:

USING THE CHECKLIST, PROCARE HAD THE FOLLOWING ANTI-PATTERNS:

Anarchy

x Anxiety

x Confusion

Politics

Chaos

x Division

During the engagement Procare closed one low-performing division so top line revenue grew from 2.5 million to 2.1 million (Yes, we know that revenue went down but it sounded clever to state it in terms of growth). Profit went from a negative $250,000 to a positive $300,000 over the course of the year.

As we have shared in all of the other mini-cases, when Flow is properly implemented the following formula describes the results:

Vision + Right People + Definitions + Distillation (of Agreements) + Delivery + Drive (to Success) = Successful Organization.

The "as is" starting point and the "to be" ending point of the effort at Procare was going to be a challenge because of the critical nature of the prior year's financial losses.

So, what changed?

A lot.

Three of the four areas of the I, We, It and Its needed attention.

I - PEOPLE (USE THE 4R AND 4D MODELS)

First, Dirk and two of his sons, Dirk III and Kyle (who now own the company) are very coachable servant leaders who were willing to listen and adapt to the changes that rose-up and were agreed to.

WE - TEAM LEVEL (USE THE 4D MODEL)

A key point regarding the success of Procare is how they live out their values. One of Dirk III's children has Down's Syndrome. This incurable genetic caused disability requires a lifetime of increased attention and care. Dirk III and his family continually exhibit love and commitment to the wider community in how they walk through life with this child.

During the time of this engagement Dirk Senior and his wife decided to adopt a Down's child from China. Dirk was in his 50s at that point. This unity of family purpose demonstrated by a radical act of compassion is amazing in today's world of "its all about me" attitudes and actions.

Obviously, these underlying values serve the Bakhuyzen family and their business well. This is fundamental to their success.

IT - PRODUCT / PROGRAM (USE THE 4D MODEL AND THE 4 WHYS)

During the Definition work, we identified that the majority of the financial losses were tied to one division. Thus, the decision was made to close the landscape construction portion of the business. Later, in the consulting process, Ted introduced the owner of a tree service company to Dirk. Procare acquired the company and hired the owner to run a tree service division, which became immediately profitable for Procare.

ITS - EXECUTIVE / PORTFOLIO (USE THE 4D MODEL, VSPT AND CASCADING VISION)

Finally, the use of our simple, powerful leadership framework allowed a continuous focus on the most important and valuable things. The small to large incremental changes became possible by focusing Procare on their weekly 2" dominoes (see the section on Cascading Vision at the beginning of Chapter 2).

Some were tried and discarded.

Others were tried and expanded.

The aggregate total result being an amazing turnaround.

SIDE NOTE: The youngest Kallman sibling, Steven John Kallman, was Down's Syndrome. He died of Leukemia when he was eight years old. We understand, to a much lesser degree, the path both Dirk's are on and they, like any parent with a disabled child, are heroes (not just in our book) in any book.

14. Mini-case: The next example is yours!
(Value-add: _____ / Industry: _____)

This is your opportunity to choose a successful project / product that you've done in the past and use the Vision Flow checklist along with the I, We, It and Its 4-box to fill in the details of that success. Use the other case studies (the 13 mini-cases along with the SingTel example) as templates when filling in your example.

This is a powerful exercise that we use in our FCP and FCT training that moves the content of this book from the abstract and theoretical over to the street-level, battle scarred arena of real-world implementations and change management.

Begin with the checklist:

USING THE CHECKLIST, PROJECT "_____
_____" HAD THE FOLLOWING ANTI-PATTERNS:

___ Anarchy

___ Anxiety

___ Confusion

___ Politics

___ Chaos

___ Division

Remember that a successful project will have had:

Vision + Right People + Definitions + Distillation (of Agreements) + Delivery + Drive (to Success) = Successful Organization. This about the "as is" starting point and the "to be" ending point of the effort. Write your thoughts here:

_____

_____

_____

_____

Now, fill in the details of your project / product for the "I, We, It and Its" 4-Box:

I - PEOPLE (USE THE 4R AND 4D MODELS)

_____   _____

_____   _____

_____   _____   _____

_____   _____

WE - TEAM LEVEL (USE THE 4D MODEL)

_____   _____

_____   _____

_____   _____   _____

_____   _____

IT - PRODUCT / PROGRAM (USE THE 4D MODEL AND THE 4 WHYS)

_____ _____

_____ _____

_____ _____ _____

_____ _____

ITS - EXECUTIVE / PORTFOLIO (USE THE 4D MODEL, VSPT AND CASCADING VISION)

_____ _____

_____ _____

_____ _____ _____

_____ _____

Write any additional thoughts here (i.e. how "Getting to Aha!" will have impacted the above 4-box, etc.):

_____

_____

_____

_____

Appendix B

Using Flow to Govern Agile

Portfolio, Program and Project / Team Governance

We have found that companies can be hesitant to get started with transitioning and/or transforming their Traditional Governance to Agile Governance for their organizations since they are unsure of where to start. There are several paths that will get you to the same destination, but we use the following outline for the journey to Agile and Flow Governance:

- Begin with the Leadership Teams
    - o Current state / Future state assessments
        - ▪ "As is" to "to be" for achieving organizational Flow
        - ▪ Uses interviews and workshops
        - ▪ Flow Road Map creation
        - ▪ From half-day to multiple week formats
    - o Cascading Vision Workshop
        - ▪ This is designed to facilitate the Leadership Team in Defining and agreeing upon the Definition for each team member's Vision for their business and technology teams.
        - ▪ Half-day format

- Facilitator-led, hands-on participative format
- The output of this workshop are the Visions that will be used to guide each of the Portfolios, Programs and Projects/Teams that work with each member of the Leadership Team

☐ Walkabout Workshop (Big Room Planning)

- o After the Vision(s) is in place, the next step is to build the "big picture" by bringing all of the teams together to product the Portfolio View
- o Full-day format
- o Facilitator-led, hands-on participative format … includes both the Leadership Team and all teams involved in Delivering the Portfolio
- o The output of this workshop is the big picture, i.e. Portfolio View

☐ The Cutting Room floor exercise (facilitated cage fight/Portfolio Prioritization)

- o Once the Portfolio View is in place, then the Leadership Team and Teams prioritize the work in the portfolio and create work in process limits for each Portfolio, Program and Project/Team
- o The Portfolio is balanced against the organization's velocity using this exercise
- o Two-day format
- o Facilitator-led, hands-on participative format --- includes both the Leadership Team and all teams involved in Delivering the Portfolio
- o The output of this exercise is the Prioritization of all work included for the Portfolios, Programs and Projects/Teams that is balanced with the existing organizational velocity

☐ Ongoing tailored solutions, including the training, coaching and mentoring of the Leadership Teams and all teams involved in Delivering the Portfolios.

- o Tailored solutions for each organization's specific situation, can include:
- o Structuring and/or setting-up an Agile PMO
- o Structuring and/or setting-up an Agile Governance Group (AGG) or Agile Transformation Group (ATG) --- used in parallel with the Agile PMO
- o Refining and/or transforming the organization's existing Governance meeting structure to an Agile Cadence
- o Creating the Agile Communication / Reporting dashboards
- o This step includes both longer-term implementations and health-checks on a regular cadence (when up and running with the customized solution that fits the needs and culture of the organization)
- ☐ Workshop(s) to sort the organization's development teams into persistent, dedicated teams
  - o Think of it like a World Cup high-performing soccer ("football" in the rest of the world) team
    - ▪ The coaches seldom substitute players when the team is out on the pitch during the game
  - o When the teams are dedicated, over time, the team's "costs" become (and behave like) fixed costs
    - ▪ This simplifies the budgeting process
  - o Quality, stability and maturity also becomes emergent when the teams are stable
  - o This enables balancing of organizational capacity and demand
    - ▪ Team members are not moved from team-to-team, but rather the work is scheduled into the team's flow of work

If you're still unsure of where to begin, then you'll want to be in touch with a Flow Certified Professional and/or Flow Certified Trainer to arrange for a customized assessment of your organization's readiness to implement Agile and Flow Governance.

Culture Makes or Breaks your Transformation

One of the primary reasons Scaling Agile is so difficult is Culture. Yes, we know the list of other reasons is long, but this one is most important.

Let's be a little realistic for a moment.

It's a pretty good bet that not all of us get to work for Spotify, King, Google, Amazon; or, for any of the other lean start-ups that have integrated Agile into their Culture right from the start. Most of us work for organizations where the Culture has emerged over years, if not decades and in some cases, it has developed over even much longer periods of time. The paths and patterns have worked and have now ossified.

And, even for those working within an organization that has tried to be truly Agile from the beginning, our gut feeling is that there is a threshold at which the fast growth of the start-up slams into a wall of reality; and, the young start-ups, or successful internal Agile teams, discover the Agile framework they started with, that was amazingly good at the team-level, is a challenge to scale. On top of that, the Agile Culture in one organization can be very difficult to duplicate in another (especially if the other company is not Agile).

Sohrab Vossoughi hit the nail on the head in an article he wrote about copying cultures:

"'Culture' is one of those fuzzy terms that makes business analysts roll their eyes, but its true power lies in the fact that, unlike other competitive advantages, it is nearly impossible to copy, and that's what makes it the real 'secret sauce.' On the surface, culture is not that complicated: it's simply 'the things that people in an organization do without thinking, often because of a precedent set by management.' But the roots of culture go very deep." [123]

And, copying, changing and/or customizing and culture just doesn't happen by itself, either. Changing an organization's culture in a large enterprise is roughly akin to trying to steer the Queen Mary from the boiler room. It can be done, but it's not pretty to watch. And, takes a ton of extra overhead to pull off.

Further, changing the culture should not be done with a big-bang program or announced with a lot of fanfare. Done correctly, it should be imperceptible to those participating in the change and should become as natural a breathing so that down the road no one remembers how painful things used to be.

It will be rather difficult for a company to change its culture if they first do not create a culture that enables change to thrive. How do we do that? We begin with Vision. And, "VSPT" and the "one thing" are key tools for transforming a culture.

In most organizations, everyone somehow believes that People and Tasks (the "P and T") are somehow automatically ("auto-magically") linked to the company's overall Vision and Strategies (the "V and S"). The reality is that there is usually a huge chasm between these two in every enterprise --- that is why we put a line separating the "VS" from the "PT."

YOUR VISION SHOULD INCLUDE A CLEARLY DEFINED:

- **Vision** (*to be*)
- **Purpose** (*what is your White-hot Why?*)
- **Core Values & Attitudes** (*tells who we are and what we believe*)
- **Mission** (*Defines the business we are in*)
- **Goals and measurable objectives** (*concrete, measurable goals that are linked to the Vision*).

Vision, as Defined above (including Vision, Purpose, Core Values and Attitudes, Mission and Goals) includes and is part of the organization's "Culture." We call this a Culture of Vision since Vision and Culture go hand-in-hand in a high-performance organization.

For VSPT (or Agile, Scrum, Kanban, Scrumban, XP, etc.) to function properly and create the desired change and for Flow to occur in any organization you must have the right Culture in place.

This is crucial since it is a well-known adage that culture eats everything (including portfolios, products, services, programs, projects and enterprise processes) for breakfast, lunch AND dinner. And, tradition is the bulldozer plowing Culture forward; i.e. "we've always done it this way…"

As we shared in Chapter 2 on Vision, it is vital that the organization understand the iterative nature of Vision. Not only do we need to Cascade Vision and "one thing" down throughout the organization, but also we need to link it back from the bottom-up so that every level of the organization is involved in iteratively shaping the overall Vision of the enterprise.

That's the power of the two-inch domino!

Linking each organizational level's Vision to the level above it is essential for creating the feedback mechanism needed to have an iterative Vision. It also is a transparent and powerful way to have the teams involved in having a say in shaping the overall Vision of the enterprise.

This participation by the teams creates buy-in to the Vision.

The Team (including the Product Owner and ScrumMaster) needs to Define their Vision, VSPT and "one thing" right up-front if they want to have any hope of succeeding with the program, product, service, and/or result they desire to Deliver. Both the individual and the team need to align their respective VSPTs with each other and with the Product they're trying to create. As we shared in Chapter 2, VSPT Cascades along with the "one thing" and the overall "Vision" of the company:

VSPT is a key component in the 4D Model's (Define, Distill, Deliver and Drive) Definition process.

Distillation can be a stormy, chaotic process.

Getting agreement on Definitions is always a challenge, but the Distillation process is essential if the team is going to avoid falling into the trap of Groupthink. Ultimately, Vision "Drives" the Product Backlog; and, the Product Backlog should encompass the entire Product Vision.

What do Flow, Vision, VSPT and the 4D Model have to do with changing Culture or scaling Agile?

Everything.

Using Flow to change culture and/or scale Agile to the Enterprise level goes way beyond merely restructuring teams and synchronizing releases (but that does help and can be a first step in the right direction).

It's more than rewriting job descriptions (although that's part of it, too).

It's more than using Release Burnup charts to communicate progress.

Using the tools included in Flow and the Unified Vision Framework, or any other Vision clarifying model, and then implementing correctly, will help create a truly Vision-led Culture where good people are free to create outstanding value. This enables the transformation of a Culture with less heartburn than normal.

Team-level Agile vs. Enterprise Agile and Flow

The differences between team-level Agile and Enterprise Agile is an uncomfortable area that isn't being adequately addressed by the Agile community. Many consultants, coaches and practitioners truly believe that Agile Coaches can scale team-level Agile to the Enterprise with minor adjustments. In some cases, that might be true, but it is not a universal Truth. However, there is a risk that the remaining part of this section may offend those who hold these beliefs.

Arthur Shopenhauer, a 19th Century German Philosopher (nicknamed "obstinate" by his detractors), once said:

"All truth goes through 3 stages. First, it is ridiculed. Second, it is violently opposed. And third, it is accepted as self-evident." [124]

So, with these disclaimers in place, the time has come for transparency regarding some of the challenges companies are facing when trying to Scale Agile.

One assumption many companies have made is that if Agile Coaches helped us become successful at the team level, then it logically follows that they should be able to help us scale Agile to the Enterprise level. That assumption may be and usually is (in our experience) deeply flawed. This is true even for companies that have started out and remain Agile.

Just because an Entrepreneurial start-up has been successfully using team-level Agile from its start-up phase **does not exempt it from basic business principles that apply to scaling all successful businesses**.

As companies grow, what worked when they had five teams suddenly no longer works with 100 teams. This is especially true from a governance perspective. It's easy to manage tribes, guilds, Scrum of Scrums, etc. when a company is small. To assume that you can successfully scale a start-up culture and its processes to the Enterprise level is naive and potentially fatal.

The reality is:

"At some point in time the Tribes need to become a Nation."

THE PMO BROTHERS

To do that, you need to have effective and focused Agile Governance for the Enterprise. We use Flow to achieve that.

If we could look behind the curtain of many Agile start-ups, we suspect that we would find a different picture than what is reported in the media. It reminds us of law 20 from the book "The 22 Immutable Laws of Marketing" (by Al Ries and Jack Trout, 1993) which had this to say about what you read in the news:

"20. *The Law of Hype*: *The situation is often the opposite of the way it appears in the press."* [125]

No Agile start-up will ever publicly admit, particularly if they are publicly traded, they are having troubles scaling Agile as they grow into more mature and larger organizations. One of the primary issues that Agile start-ups face as they grow is that they are now dealing with a completely different kind of professional stakeholder who speaks an entirely different language and has a completely different set of expectations. In many circles, we call these stakeholders "Executives."

The language difference between management and Executive leadership usually comes as a shock for the Agile and Scrum purists. They assume that success communicating at the management and team level should automatically translate into success communicating with the Executive level without any accommodation for the tribal differences. They also firmly believe that the same tools and methodologies used at the team level will work at the Executive level. We have observed that trying to force feed Scrum to traditional Executives generally ends badly.

It takes an Agile professional who possesses a high level of business acumen and maturity to be able to speak the Executive's language. It is even better if you can find an Agile professional who has been part of that tribe, i.e. one with Executive experience. Anyone who has worked at the C-level has already learned, and acknowledged, that a pragmatic, methodology agnostic approach is a more successful way of working.

By the way, the Agile and Scrum purist's "force feeding" mindset (that Scrum or Agile can only be done one way, regardless of its audience) strikes us as unusual, especially from a group of people that pride themselves on quickly adjusting and adapting to an empirical reality.

Up to this point, some Agilists reading this section may already be responding with ridicule and disdain. Others may even be responding in violent opposition to what we're saying.

But our intent is to try and explain what we have found to be clear and self-evident when successfully Scaling Agile to the Enterprise. So, before getting all riled up and shooting the messengers, please follow our observations all the way through to their final conclusion.

When talking about Agile coaching, or team facilitation, it's appropriate to be aware that almost all Agile literature and training is targeted at the individual and team level. This doesn't make it bad, but it also doesn't make it effective when trying to execute Agile in the Executive suite.

What this means in practice is that a majority of Agile Coaches can't scale and probably shouldn't.

Yes, we know it's not fair or accurate to lump all Agile Coaches together since some Agile Coaches actually have the experience, education and skill to be able to scale Agile and do it well.

The rest of this section is about why the above quote is true for the vast majority of Agile Coaches with which we have come in contact. It seems that many of the Agile Coaches themselves have missed a key point from title of the Agile Manifesto:

*"Manifesto for **Agile <u>Software</u>** Development"*

By Definition, "Agile," as described (and limited) by the Manifesto, is only for software development. It was not originally intended for the entire organization. That doesn't mean that Agile's Values and Attitudes cannot be used in other areas. But, it does mean that the signers of the Manifesto understood the limits and constraints of software development in context and relationship to the rest of the Enterprise.

There are examples of organizations that use Scrum and Agile for the entire enterprise: Salesforce.com and F-Secure to name a couple. However, the number of organizations that are struggling to scale Scrum and Agile far exceed the examples of those who have succeeded.

Most Agile Coaches and ScrumMasters are all about working with and facilitating teams (and individuals) with the goal of getting the teams to become high performing. This is part of what makes Agile and Scrum so effective.

And, Agile Coaches are taught to "lead" (train, coach and mentor) from the back of the room, as they should. For example, Lyssa Adkins book "Coaching Agile Teams," has entire chapters on the coach as a mentor, facilitator, teacher, problem-solver, conflict navigator and collaboration conductor. This makes enormous sense at the team level.

Another example is Sharon Bowman's "Training from the Back of the Room," which is the required course and book for anyone seriously considering becoming a CST (Certified Scrum Trainer).

These courses and books are both focused on training individuals and teams, not executives.

It has been our observation, however, when working at the Senior Manager, Executive and Board levels, it is an absolute requirement that a project, program and/or portfolio leader has Executive-level "room presence." Most of the Agile Coaches that we have observed in action don't possess the room presence required to effectively communicate to and interact with Executive leadership. This should not come as a surprise since they've actually been trained to do the opposite (to lead from the back of the room).

Assuming that all of the above statements are true, and even if an Agile coach has Executive level experience and/or "room presence," we have witnessed a deeper, more fundamental problem within the Agile community that is blocker to effective scaling. The following quote from a well-known Agile Coach captures the essence of this problem:

"Management is the source of all Evil in the world." "Frank" (actual name withheld to protect the less-than-innocent)

Let's be a little blunt here: statements like this are only true in the land of Dilbert's pointy-haired boss. Every organization has Appholes like this lurking in the org-chart. However, healthy mature and growing Enterprises do not hold or share this errant belief. Further, Agile and Scrum "purists" with this attitude have not done themselves (or the Agile Community at large) any favors by blaming all Agile transformation, transition and governance difficulties and/or failures on management or the leadership of the Enterprise.

This is a classic example of biting the hand that feeds you. Worse, it blocks the ability of the organization to migrate to an Agile culture and many times kills the attempted transformation effort. It is the epitome of anti-Flow.

Why is that? It's because, as we pointed out above, the language of Enterprise leadership is different than the language of management, Agile or otherwise. I (Andrew) have a perfect example of this from awhile back when I had the opportunity to attend a meeting for an Agile consulting company (that has both Agile Coaches and Agile Management Consultants).

The most fascinating, passionate discussion I've witnessed, so far, in my Agile journey, erupted during the course of this meeting. As we shared in the quote above, one of the Agile Coaches had a complete meltdown during the meeting and literally blamed "ALL Evil in the entire world on management consultants, managers and executives." Extreme? Yes. Unusual? Unfortunately, not so much.

Purist Agile Coaches tend to ferociously fight to "keep a space for Agile and Scrum" (as they have been taught to do). However, the most fascinating and rewarding part of the meeting was when the Chief Executive Officer of the company challenged and rebuked the riled-up Agile Coach with the following response in front of all of the other Agilists and Management Consultants in the room:

"Frank*, by definition, if we are doing Agile consulting with the management of a company, then we are "Agile" management consultants." [126]

The crimson-faced Agile coach sat down and the meeting continued.

Later in the same meeting, on a flip chart, the President of the company had drawn a matrix with each of their products and services that they offered their clients. The horizontal swim lanes were sorted by Portfolio, Program and Product, Project and Team and Individual Team Member levels; and, the vertical swim lanes were a categorization of their products and services. ALL of their "Agile" products and services were aimed primarily at the Project, Team and Individual levels.

However, at the Program, Portfolio and Executive levels they had little or no product offerings. No surprise there, either. Very few Agile consulting companies have any product offerings that truly meet the needs of the Executive level. Why is that? Because Agile methods began at, and are optimized for, the team (and by extension, the individual).

Andrew then went up to the flip chart and drew two boxes around the CEO's Product / Service offering matrix that looked like the following:

EXECUTIVE
SENIOR MANAGEMENT
MANAGEMENT

The above groups speak the language of leadership. And:

PROJECT
TEAM
INDIVIDUAL

The Project level to the individual level speaks the language of management.

These two groups are not necessarily speaking the same language or are necessarily aligned on the same page.

A hush fell over the room as the idea of the two languages sunk in and as they understood that Agile, for the most part, had ignored the leadership and governance levels, from both a communications and product standpoint.

Agile purists, like Frank, have done a superb job of alienating almost everyone from the middle management level on up through the Executive team in companies with which they have worked.

Worse, that particular coach wore it as a badge of honor that executives refused to meet with him; or, in the cases where they did, they never invited him back to another leadership meeting, ever. This is because Agile purists speak a language that is foreign to the pragmatic, Executive leadership of the organization and because they have a value-set that is not aligned with the Executives. It is possible to preserve a "space for Agile and Scrum" without being offensive, arrogant, rude or demeaning.

It has been suggested that, at the team level, 80% of all project management is communication. We would add that when working with the higher levels of an organization, it is nearly 100%. When Purist Agile Coaches view Senior Management, etc., as the source of all evil, then that unprofessional attitude will be communicated loud and clear to those Stakeholders and everyone with which they associate. This is not a good thing and is truly a very unproductive anti-pattern.

People seem to have forgotten a well-known adaptation of the golden rule:

"He who has the gold, rules…"

ANON

One of the religious truisms of Scrum is that teams need to be self-organized, self-managed and self-governed. However, everyone working on any Agile or Scrum product / project is accountable for the budget entrusted to them. If the team is not self-funded, then they are not truly self-governed. If they're not paying their salaries out of their own pockets, then they are financially accountable to the company and Executives that *are* funding the project team that is doing the product, service or result. And, we believe that:

"Sitting around in a circle, holding hands and singing "Kumbaya" isn't going to get a team very far with a group of jaded, "show-me-the-money" investors, Board Members and/or Executives." [127]

THE PMO BROTHERS

The team's responsibility and Mission is to Deliver an increment of value to the Product Owner who is the voice of the customer. The Product Owner is the single, wringable neck, who ultimately accepts or rejects each increment completed by the team. By the way, as often as the Agile community rails against "command-and-control" organizations, the Definition and role of the Product Owner is actually complete "command-and-control." Because the "yea-or-nay" sign-off lives with them alone. This is indeed necessary and strong control.

As we mentioned earlier, some Agile Coaches have actually started to understand aspects of successful scaling. However, assuming that Team Agile, facilitated by Agile Coaches, will automatically translate to the Enterprise level has been a painful experience for many companies.

It's not necessarily a question of Agile Coaches being able to understand the methods, frameworks, or principles of how to scale. It's a question of battle scars, skill and demonstrated previous success in scaling Agile. The universe of people that have "been there, done that" within the Agile community is rather small. That is why methodology agnostic frameworks, like Flow and the UVF, are absolutely crucial for creating an organizational culture that facilitates Agile in all quadrants.

Implementing and scaling Agile requires skilled Coaches that know how and when to use the right tool for the right situation. During the past 2 decades, we have found that the Flow, the UVF and the VSPT, 4D and 4R Models will focus your organization to optimize all four areas, the "I, We, It and Its" lenses, that all Enterprise Agile must address.

"Enterprises do not scale from the bottom up. Scaling occurs from the top and bottom, simultaneously, using Vision." [128]

THE PMO BROTHERS

Agile Coaches that only have a software development background usually do not have anywhere near the education, business experience and/or skills at the Executive level to Deliver what is needed. Hoping your Agile Coaches, using an organic "team" Agile approach, will get you to Enterprise "scaled Agile" simply won't cut it.

Cultural Change and Why Scaling Agile is Really, Really Tough

The myth that Agile Can't Scale has been floating around for a couple of years now. But that is true if you Define "Agile" as a team-level methodology, then we'll be a little provocative here and suggest that in this case Team Agile **is not scalable**. That's our observation having worked with Agile PMO and Portfolio Management for the better part of the last decade with a number of companies. We've watched more than one company crash and burn attempting to scale using Team Agile.

On the other hand, if you are Defining "Agile" as an organizational-level methodology like Flow, then we not only suggest that Agile is scalable, we absolutely know for a fact that it is … since we've successfully done it, hands-on, for a number of organizations.

In the case of Team Agile, we have observed that there a point in time that the explosive growth of an Agile start-up far outpaces the ability of the organization's founders to continue on a productive path. There usually is a point in time that a start-up's growth curve outstrips a founder's ability to lead a maturing organization.

That is the mistake many organizations are making. Instead, they should be looking at it holistically and use a Flow framework like the UVF since it is designed to scale Agile to the entire Enterprise.

First, we should probably differentiate what we mean between Team Agile and Flow.

As the description implies, Team Agile is Agile that is used at the team level. This would include Agile tools and methodologies like Scrum, XP, Kanban, Scrumban, etc. Each one of these tools is optimized for single teams of 7 people, +/- 2, etc.

Flow, on the other hand, extends beyond the Agile Team to the entire organization. It includes the balance of Business Content and Leadership that is not naturally or normally involved at the team level where, typically, the Product Owner is the Voice of the Customer (and the balance of the organization). The reason Team Agile works so well at the team level is that it limits the team size and thus reduces the number of communication channels and it allows intrinsic motivations to drive team success. The same idea applies to Flow for the Enterprise, but for other reasons.

Moving from Team Agile to Flow is a journey.

At the beginning of the journey, the risk is higher and the value-added can be lower. As the organization matures, it learns how to mitigate risk and higher value is added. All businesses, whether they started out Agile or not, go through a process similar to this. Let's focus on the journey from Team Agile to Flow, which mirrors the voyage from lower value-add to higher value-add.

Somewhere along the way, usually between "Entrepreneur" and "Producer," an organization will begin to experience growing pains. Even companies that started out "Agile" right from the start will not be immune to this. Some will try to avoid scaling since they don't believe it's necessary. So, they do everything in their power to shield the teams from having to deal with a new layer of organizational complexity that they believe adds little to no value. And, for those companies transitioning from a Waterfall to Agile culture, there is more work to be done on this trip (than a start-up). Without dramatic, excellent leadership, it can take between five to seven years to move into a fully functioning Flow culture. Flow, properly implemented and led, can help an organization shorten the length of this journey.

Scrum, or team Agile, has been optimized and proven successful for the team level. Flow is optimized and has demonstrated extraordinary success for the Enterprise. Using Flow, Programs and Portfolios are self-organized and self-governed at the Executive and Senior Management levels. And thus, Flow optimizes the divisions, functional areas, teams and individuals as well.

The very nature of fast growing organizations is hierarchical, even if they grew organically from the start. Team Agile will work well in small settings from the Visionary start-up up through to somewhere around the Entrepreneurial level as described above. There is, however, a point where the growth of the organization exceeds its ability to retain the original start-up and entrepreneurial cultures that made them such fun and dynamic places at which to work. It is at that point that employing a simple structure for scaling Flow is necessary. The idea is simple, but simple is not easy. In fact, it is time consuming and in some cases, excruciatingly painful. Wisdom and patience, when implementing Flow, are truly important virtues.

The key thing is to implement Flow Program and Portfolio Governance in a way that doesn't disturb the organization's existing Agile culture. The risk here is that an organization overreacts to the change and ends up stifling Team Agile by placing layers of complexity on it that add little or no value to what the organization is really trying to achieve. One of the main reasons the additional complexity fails to fix complicated organizational issues is the "disconnect between the VS and PT in every organization.

Team Agile is a great place to start for any organization that wants to enjoy the value and benefits that Agile can add. For those that want to scale agile to the next level, to what we call Enterprise Flow, it will take more than the tools used to manage the team level. The Program and Portfolio levels both have a cadence that is slower than the project / team level. Aligning these cadences means that you'll have three, very different backlogs to manage and implement:

- ☐ The Portfolio Backlog is comprised of Epics
- ☐ The Program Backlog is comprised of Sub-Epics and/or Features
- ☐ The Product Backlog at the team / project level typically has User Stories, but can also have other types of Product Backlog Items

As we've stated in the past, the Product Backlog should encompass the entire Vision of the Product. In the same way, the Program and Portfolio Backlogs should encompass the entire Vision for each of those levels as well. The management of these Backlogs are the heart and soul of Flow Program and Portfolio governance.

These Backlogs need to be constructed in a way so that they do not disturb the team-level culture and it is import to recognize and understand that the cadences for each of these levels are different. It involves a lot of simplification, forced prioritization, and removing a large number of the "templates" that a PMO would be tempted to use from traditional PPM. It is also essential to Define the organizational level Vision and KPIs that will be used to lead and manage the Programs and Portfolios.

Flow **is scalable,** as long as your organization is willing to take a holistic, long-term view on how to get from Vision to a Scaled Enterprise.

Our view is that Flow is the next wave and Flow can heal the rift between Teams and Management that was inadvertently created by well-meaning (but misguided) Agile "purists" that really didn't understand the roadmap required to Scale Agile.

Although 58% of all Agile projects fail according to Dr. Sutherland (co-creator of Scrum), this level of failure is three times better than traditional methodologies that fail at a rate as much as 86% of the time. However, we believe that a 58% failure rate is still unacceptable. We also believe that a limitation to better success rates is the inability of organizations to scale, causing friction and dissonance that is unnecessary and counterproductive.

It has been said that 80% of all project management is communications. We agree. It is time to communicate how to bridge the cultural gap from entrepreneurial start-up to mature operational excellence. This requires leadership and a simple framework. We have found that using a lean, Flow leadership framework like the UVF is the fastest and easiest way to accomplish it.

The Three Journeys to a truly Flow Culture

"Traditional/Waterfall projects have a success rate of 14% and Agile/Scrum projects have a success rate of 42%." [129]

DR. JEFF SUTHERLAND

There are usually three (or more) change management journeys on which a company will embark on its way to becoming a Flow Culture. This section is divided into three interrelated journeys:

- ☐ The Journey of **Investing in Prioritization and People**
- ☐ The Journey to **Excellence and Professionalism**
- ☐ The Journey to a **High-Performance, Flow Culture**

As with any journey, there are bumps along the way and occasionally we crash into the ditch on the side of the road. This is a candid and pragmatic view derived from successful journeys other organizations have come through.

Welcome to the first journey… the **Journey of Investing in Prioritization and People.**

Even though Agile triples the success rate as compared to traditional methods, it's still under 50% success overall (i.e. completing the project on-time, on-budget and in-scope), so there is always room for improvement.

One of the classic, all-time "project" failures was the Sidney Opera House. The project was completed ten years late and over-budget by more than fourteen times! By any measure, that project was a utter failure:

- ☐ The original cost estimate in 1957 was $7 million
- ☐ The final cost was $102 million
- ☐ The original completion date set by the government was 26 January 1963
- ☐ The Opera House was formally completed in 1973

If the story ended there, it would be a sad one.

However, "in 2012 the total economic revenue generated by this iconic structure was $123,696,000. In 2012 Sydney Opera House Trust had 847 employees in Australia including employees from all subsidiaries under the company's control." [130]

That's just one year of operations. Since 1973 the Sidney Opera House has generated Billions in revenue and has gone from being a complete failure, from a project perspective, to being one of the most stellar product successes in modern history.

There are many tools that can be used to try to determine the value of a project before it's started, including ROI (return on investment), IRR (internal rate of return) and Value-add. Of these three, value-add is probably one of the best since it answers the three "whys" (i.e. why are we doing this project)?

There are only four (4) reasons to do a portfolio, product, program, project:

1. Increase Revenues
2. Decrease Costs
3. Mitigate or eliminate risk
4. Do the right thing

Having the right level of Flow governance for your portfolio of programs and projects is a mixture of art and science. The Sydney Opera House is a classic example of keeping the long-term Product Vision in sight in spite of the difficulties encountered at the Project/Team level.

Many CEO's are beginning to take a long-term, Agile approach for their organizations and that's what this new journey is all about. It's the same journey that many companies have been on for the past decade. But, instead of trying to scale Agile to the Enterprise level, perhaps it would be better to start at the top of the organization and use Flow instead.

It's always a challenge for any company to wisely invest in the right Portfolio of Programs / Products and Projects. One of the first exercises that we did with the key the key stakeholders for one organization (a Fortune 50 company) with which we worked was to go through the Portfolio Backlog of Prioritized Projects:

- ☐ We had around 14 key Programs in the pipeline in for 2014 and 2015
- ☐ We worked on determining the bandwidth of the organization needed to be able to carry out all of the work generated by these 14 Programs
- ☐ The second part of the exercise was to have the key stakeholders do what we called the "cutting room floor" exercise
    - o The bandwidth (i.e. development team's capacity) was reconciled and balanced with the work/demand; and, items not immediately needed were deleted / adjusted from the Portfolio
    - o Although all 14 key programs were "must do," some are more "must do" than others and would need to be prioritized as the year progressed
    - o And, only those key programs deemed to be of the highest value for each key stakeholder's area would be completed during 2014

The resulting prioritized Portfolio Backlog represented the projects that could be completed during the 12 - 24-month period from Q1 of 2014 through the end of Q4 2015. We completed the Backlog. The value-add of the cutting room floor exercise was immense since it pared down the work to the most important Programs/Projects. This created a sustainable rate that matched each team's velocity/capacity to the demand.

And teams are made up of **People** (the "P" in VSPT).

The competition in the marketplace for seasoned and skilled Agile team members is getting fierce. The undersupply of qualified, experienced Agile leaders is one of the things contributing to a large number of Scaled Agile change efforts that just don't produce the intended results (or, flat-out fail!).

We have observed that there is a severe undersupply of seasoned Product Owners that are qualified to lead Agile projects or who could assist at the organizational and enterprise level.

"A study conducted by Yoh based on data from CareerBuilder's Supply and Demand Portal revealed that the number of advertised agile jobs outnumbered active candidates by 4.59-to-1." [131]

That's almost a 5 to 1 ratio of Agile jobs open to active candidates that are available. The Yoh report also stated that,

"This skills gap has not only made it difficult for companies to quickly source quality talent on demand, but also puts them at risk of hiring technical professionals that have poor agile methodology skills." [132]

Companies may intuitively understand the need to go Agile, but in most cases, are not prepared for the ferocious competition for top notch Agile talent. And, if they need to scale their efforts at the same time, then that exponentially increases the fight for top talent. Training will be a core need.

The journey continues with the **Journey to Excellence and Professionalism.**

"A journey of a thousand miles begins with a single step." [133]

CHINESE PROVERB

It is always good to emphasize the need for a higher level of professionalism and discipline. The first step on the journey to a higher level of professionalism is training. And, as you have learned in this book, Flow goes beyond Agile. We have recently launched two certifications:

☐ FCP - Flow Certified Professional
☐ FCT - Flow Certified Trainer

If your company desires to take Agile and Flow beyond your IT and Technology departments, then you will want to seriously consider training your people in Flow.

There is an old management joke about investing in training that goes something like, "what if we invest in training and/or certifying our people and they leave; but, what if we don't and they stay?" Training should not be an option; it is a must-have. Training and certifications are only the first couple of steps in this journey.

In their book on agile ("Software in 30 Days"), Sutherland and Schwaber (the co-creators of Scrum) have now begun to let companies know that it takes up to five to seven years to complete a Waterfall to Agile transformation. That is the Definition of a long, onerous and sometimes dangerous journey! And, as we shared earlier, Flow can dramatically reduce the time required for successful transformation.

It's not just the teams that have to make the leap.

As we shared earlier in the book with the I, We, It and Its and the Aha! Curve, every individual must successfully make the personal transition from legacy command-and-control thinking (i.e. waterfall /traditional) to embrace an Agile mindset.

The magnitude of the Cultural shift required to move from traditional to Agile can be immense. It is very encouraging to hear that many of our client's leadership are embracing and espousing Agile and Lean thinking and are Cascading that Vision throughout their organizations. Agile concepts are deceptively simple. But, "simple is not easy" and that has been our message during the past decades.

Being Agile and Lean requires a higher level of personal and team discipline (and professionalism) than what was previously found or required in typical traditional/waterfall PM approaches and organizations.

The journey's getting longer with the Drive required to achieve a **High-Performance, Flow Culture.**

"Culture eats 'process' for breakfast..." [134]

JOHN DEHART

There is a risk that companies potentially miss the most important opportunity when they make organizational changes --- that is, making the necessary changes to the culture to position it for the future. In a recent post on Scrum Inc.'s Blog, Steve Denning observed:

"…when the culture doesn't fit Agile, the solution is not to reject Agile. The solution is to change the organizational culture. One doesn't even have to look at the business results of firms using hierarchical bureaucracy to know that they are fatally ill. In today's marketplace, they will need to change their culture or they will die. They need to become Agile." [135]

We shared earlier the success and failure rates for Agile projects. Our suspicion is that the low rates of success are due to companies jumping on the "Agile" bandwagon without first fully grasping the Cultural change that is required from the very top on down. John Dehart summed it up perfectly with his observation as to why Southwest's competitors failed when they tried to copy Southwest's success:

"…they failed because you can copy all of the business strategies all you want, but if you don't have the culture to execute, you won't succeed. We love the line 'Culture eats process for breakfast.' Southwest Airlines has mastered culture building." [136]

Creating culture change can be a long, arduous trek. It requires that senior and executive management learn a whole new way to lead and manage the organization. The first step on that path is that every Board Member, Executive and Senior manager in the organization takes the two-day Flow Certified Professional (FCP) training.

Without the ability to see the organization through the lens of an FCP that is trained in Flow, then there is the risk of losing out on realizing the full value-add and potential of Flow. It requires a long-term view, leadership and persistence to fully implement Flow. It may happen quickly doing it on your own, but you cannot count on that.

To implement a Flow Culture requires a higher level of trust than what is normal in traditional settings. Accountability and transparency are two of the key benefits of having a Flow culture.

To achieve a Flow Culture means that we re-examine the ideas we previously used in a traditional, waterfall (i.e. date-driven, etc.) setting. The road map to being truly Flow optimized can take you through some very uncomfortable territory.

Having worked with many organizations making the transformation from waterfall to Agile and ultimately to Flow, the common theme is that the same type of situations (or heartburn) emerge at almost the exact same time during each company's journey.

And, the common denominator determining the success or failure of your journey will be the clarity of your Vision boiled down to the actionable "One Thing" and 2" domino. This will Drive cultural change.

By the way, It's been 15 years since the original "Manifesto for Agile Software Development" was forged on February 12, 2001, by 17 software development leaders. The pace of change continues to accelerate and Agile Methodologies have begun the long journey to replicate themselves beyond software and IT.

Recently Andrew was chatting with some of his colleagues in Stockholm, Sweden and they had suggested creating a new Manifesto that deals with Scaling Agile. It was during one of the discussions on this topic that Andrew pointed out that there is actually a subtle, yet key, difference between Scaling Agile and Agile Governance. And, so far, it has been a really tough sell for the Technology side of the company to convince the Business side of the organization to adopt "Agile." The graphic below helps describe the issue:

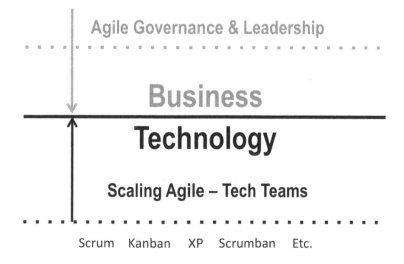

Scaling Agile has primarily been limited to all activities below the line in the Technology area. Governance, on the other hand, is above the line and impacts the entire organization. To date, Agile has grown organically from the bottom-up.

There are a myriad of team-level tools like Scrum, Kanban, XP, Scrumban, etc. And, for scaling technology teams and programs there are tools like SAFe, DAD, LeSS, etc. But, they all are targeted at the technology side of the house. Management 3.0 sort of straddles the line between technology and business, but it is primarily aimed at and utilized on the Technology side (for the middle-layer of management).

Flow and the Unified Vision Framework, begins with the Executive in mind. But also, due to its simplicity, it also works at the team-level, regardless of the methodology.

We believe it is time to initiate the discussion about a Manifesto for Agile Governance instead of just for Scaling Agile. This is because we feel that a Manifesto that could be used for just Scaling Agile, for example, would limit the discussion to only Technology and not through a management lens. In our opinion, a Manifesto for Agile Governance raises the discussion to the Executive and leadership levels in the organization.

A number of well known, authors and experts in the Agile community have recently published books on how to scale Agile and Scrum to the Enterprise level. We find it interesting that a Manifesto for either Scaling Agile or Agile Governance hasn't yet been agreed upon (or even brought up) by anyone else in the Agile community.

So, to get the ball rolling, we propose the following new Manifesto for Agile Governance for consideration:

MANIFESTO FOR AGILE GOVERNANCE

We are uncovering better ways of delivering business value
by doing it and helping others do it.
Through this work, we have come to value:
Clear Vision and Strategy over *team-level, or individual, self-prioritization*
Servant leadership over *micromanaging, command and control*

Business value delivered over *completed product, service or result*
Stakeholder collaboration over *unbending governance structures*
Iteratively leading change & innovation over *following rigid plans*
That is, while there may be value in doing the items on the right,
we value delivering the items on the left more.

So, why propose a Manifesto for Agile Governance when Flow actually goes beyond Agile? Because we believe that the iterative nature of Agile and Agile Governance will eventually enable companies to get to where we are now with Flow. And there are many steps in the journey of a thousand miles. This is just one of the steps.

A clear, Cascaded Vision, knowing and focusing on your "One Thing," identifying and doing your 2" domino in short cycles and small batches while keeping the most important things visible, will lead you and your organization into a high-performing state of Flow.

Acknowledgements

First and foremost, we would like to thank God and express our thanks and deepest gratitude to our wives, Claudia (Ted) and Gunilla (Andrew), our families, siblings and parents. Without you, this incredible journey is meaningless.

We would like to thank and gratefully acknowledge the individuals with which we've worked, trained, coached and mentored during these past three decades. It is from all of you that we have Distilled, refined and honed the UVF and Flow. We would like to specifically thank the FCP (Flow Certified Professional) and FCT (Flow Certified Trainer) participants in Stockholm, Sweden and Grand Rapids, Michigan that helped us refine and clarify Flow.

We would like to express our many thanks to our wives, our sister Mary, Jeff Kissinger, and the small army of team members that helped proofread this book and for the excellent feedback they shared with us. We appreciate your time, input and encouragement to make this book even better.

Lastly, we would like to thank you, the reader for investing the time and effort in getting into learning how to get into the Flow

Contact the PMO Brothers

For more information about the co-authors, or if you would like more information about how to implement Flow and the Unified Vision Framework in your organization, see our websites at:

www.pmobrothers.com

pmobrothers.wordpress.com

www.unifiedvisiongroup.com

www.nehemiaheffect.com

Contact Ted at

ted@unifiedvisiongroup.com

Contact Andrew at:

andrew@unifiedvisiongroup.com

Footnotes and References

Introduction Footnotes

1   Jack Welch in http://www.slideshare.net/dandoe/agile-beyond-software, slide 7

2   Peter Diamandis, in his weekly technology email blast on 10 January 2016.

3   Mihaly Csikszentmihalyi in "Good Business: Leadership, Flow, and the Making of Meaning" Penguin Group, 2003, page 203

4   Gary Hamel in "The Future of Management" Harvard Business School Press, 2007, page 58

5   Gary Hamel in "The Future of Management" Harvard Business School Press, 2007, page 59

6   See http://bleacherreport.com/articles/2605673-overlooked-kirk-cousins-has-studied-his-way-to-the-top-of-the-game

7   See http://www.amazon.com/Insanity-Albert-Einstein-motivational-poster/dp/B00W61BTYM

8   Gary Hamel in "The Future of Management" Harvard Business School Press, 2007, page 35

9   Ted and Andrew Kallman in "The Nehemiah Effect: Ancient Wisdom from the World's First Agile Projects" Xulon Press, 2014, Page xv

10   Wall Street Journal, Vol. CCLXIX No. 11 Sat/Sun Jan 14-15, 2017, page A11

Preface Footnotes

11   Colin Powell in http://www.goodreads.com/quotes/313423-a-dream-doesn-t-become-reality-through-magic-it-takes-sweat

Chapter 1 Footnotes

12   From a 1911 newspaper article quoting newspaper editor Tess Flanders https://en.wikipedia.org/wiki/A_picture_is_worth_a_thousand_words

13   Mihaly Csikszentmihalyi in "Drive: the Surprising Truth about what Motivates Us" Penguin Group, 2009, pages 112 and 113

14   Mihaly Csikszentmihalyi in "Flow: the Psychology of Optimal Experience" Harper Perennial, 1990, page 42

15   Daniel Pink in "Drive: the Surprising Truth about what Motivates Us" Penguin Group, 2009, page 116 - 117

16   David Allen in "Getting Things Done: The Art of Stress-Free Productivity," Viking / Penguin Group, 2001, page 10

17   Craig Lambert in "Getting Things Done: The Art of Stress-Free Productivity," Viking / Penguin Group, 2001, page 10

18   Steven Kotler with Peter Diamandis in their book "Bold: How to Go Big, Create Wealth and Impact the World" Simon and Schuster, 2015, page 86

19   Donald Reinertsen in "The Principles of Product Development Flow" Celeritas Publishing, 2009, pages 2, 3 and 10

20   Steven Kotler with Peter Diamandis in their book "Bold: How to Go Big, Create Wealth and Impact the World" Simon and Schuster, 2015, page 91

21   Jim Collins and William Lazier in "Beyond Entrepreneurship" Prentice Hall, 1992, page 20

22   David Allen in "Getting Things Done: The Art of Stress-Free Productivity," Viking / Penguin Group, 2001, page 19

23   Warren Buffet in http://joshkaufman.net/warren-buffett-on-business-schools/

Chapter 2 Footnotes - Elements of Flow

24   Steve Jobs in "Wired," 19.12.2012, pg. 233

25   Peter Drucker in http://www.motivateus.com/leadership-quotes-for-executives.htm

26   David Marquet in"Turn the Ship Around!" Penguin Group, 2012, page 46

27   Gary Hamel in "The Future of Management" Harvard Business School Press, 2007, page 77

28   Gary Hamel in "The Future of Management" Harvard Business School Press, 2007, page 136

29   Ted and Andrew Kallman in "The Nehemiah Effect: Ancient Wisdom from the World's First Agile Projects" Xulon Press, 2014, Page 57

30   Vincent van Gogh, see: https://www.brainyquote.com/quotes/quotes/v/vincentvan120866.html

31   Daniel Pink in "Drive: the Surprising Truth about what Motivates Us" Penguin Group, 2009, page 108

32   Gallup Business Journal, 02 Nov 2010, see: http://www.gallup.com/businessjournal/144140/Leading-Engagement-Top.aspx?utm_source=

33   Gallup Business Journal, 02 Nov 2010, see: http://www.gallup.com/businessjournal/144140/Leading-Engagement-Top.aspx?utm_source=

34   Gallup Business Journal, 02 April 2015, see: http://www.gallup.com/businessjournal/182228/managers-engaged-jobs.aspx?utm_source=cascade%20effect&utm_medium=search&utm_campaign=tiles

35   Gallup Business Journal, 02 April 2015, see: http://www.gallup.com/businessjournal/182228/managers-engaged-jobs.aspx?utm_source=cascade%20effect&utm_medium=search&utm_campaign=tiles

36   David Marquet in"Turn the Ship Around!" Penguin Group, 2012, page 60

37   The PMO Brothers, aka Ted and Andrew Kallman, in "The Nehemiah Effect: Ancient Wisdom from the World's First Agile Projects" Xulon Press, 2014, Pages 45-46

38   Jim Collins and William Lazier in "Beyond Entrepreneurship" Prentice Hall, 1992, page 192

39   Aaron Shenhar and Dov Dvir in "Reinventing Project Management" Harvard Business School Press, 2006, page 7

40   Steven Kotler with Peter Diamandis in their book "Bold: How to Go Big, Create Wealth and Impact the World" Simon and Schuster, 2015, page 119

41   Gary Hamel in "The Future of Management" Harvard Business School Press, 2007, page 62

42   Gary Hamel in "The Future of Management" Harvard Business School Press, 2007, page 87

43   Jim Collins and William Lazier in "Beyond Entrepreneurship" Prentice Hall, 1992, page 190

44   Jim Collins and William Lazier in "Beyond Entrepreneurship" Prentice Hall, 1992, pages 35-36

45   Donald Reinertsen in "The Principles of Product Development Flow" Celeritas Publishing, 2009, page 9

46   Donald Reinertsen in "The Principles of Product Development Flow" Celeritas Publishing, 2009, page 11

47   Donald Reinertsen in "The Principles of Product Development Flow" Celeritas Publishing, 2009, page 14

48   Donald Reinertsen in "The Principles of Product Development Flow" Celeritas Publishing, 2009, page 13 *see also: http://dw2blog.com/2012/01/01/ planning-for-optimal-flow-in-an-uncertain-world/*

49   Rob Flaherty in a Blog Post from March 2014, http://parsnip.io/blog/ proxy-variables/

50   Jim Collins and William Lazier in "Beyond Entrepreneurship" Prentice Hall, 1992, page 57

51   Peter Drucker in "The Leader's Guide to Radical Management" Josse Bass / John Wiley and Sons, 2010, page 23

52   Simon Cinek in "Start with WHY" Penguin Group, 2009, page 79

53   See also: http://www.sermoncentral.com/pastors-preaching-articles/bill-hybels-bill-hybels-do-you-have-a-white-hot-vision-1493.asp and https://twitter.com/wcagls/status/629302052343128064 and http://www.churchleaders.com/daily-buzz/259838-intangibles-leadership-bill-hybels-2015-summit-begun.html

54   David Marquet in "Turn the Ship Around!" Penguin Group, 2012, page 46

55   See Lyssa Adkins' and David Spayd's updated slide deck at: http://www. slideshare.net/agileindia/windows-on-transformation-montreal-2-distibution by David Spayd and Lyssa Adkins

56   Donald Reinertsen in "The Principles of Product Development Flow" Celeritas Publishing, 2009, pages 17 – 18 and 113

57   Donald Reinertsen in "The Principles of Product Development Flow" Celeritas Publishing, 2009, page 10

58   Donald Reinertsen in "The Principles of Product Development Flow" Celeritas Publishing, 2009, page 111

59   David Robertson in "Brick by Brick: How LEGO Rewrote the Rules of Innovation and Conquered the Global Toy Industry" Crown Publishing Group, a Division of Random House, 2013, page 108

60   David Robertson in "Brick by Brick: How LEGO Rewrote the Rules of Innovation and Conquered the Global Toy Industry" Crown Publishing Group, a Division of Random House, 2013, page 116

61   Donald Reinertsen in "The Principles of Product Development Flow" Celeritas Publishing, 2009, page 129

62   Donald Reinertsen in "The Principles of Product Development Flow" Celeritas Publishing, 2009, pages 36-37.

63   Jim Collins and William Lazier in "Beyond Entrepreneurship" Prentice Hall, 1992, page 173

64   Jim Collins and William Lazier in "Beyond Entrepreneurship" Prentice Hall, 1992, page 216

65   David Marquet in "Turn the Ship Around!" Penguin Group, 2012, page 54

66   David Marquet in "Turn the Ship Around!" Penguin Group, 2012, page 20

67   Mihaly Csikszentmihalyi in "Good Business: Leadership, Flow, and the Making of Meaning" Penguin Group, 2003, page 120

Chapter 3 Footnotes - Why use Flow?

68 Aaron Shenhar and Dov Dvir in "Reinventing Project Management" Harvard Business School Press, 2006, page 8

69   David Robertson in "Brick by Brick: How LEGO Rewrote the Rules of Innovation and Conquered the Global Toy Industry" Crown Publishing Group, a Division of Random House, 2013, page 118

70   David Marquet in "Turn the Ship Around!" Penguin Group, 2012, page 52

71 Dr. John Kotter, Harvard Business School, in a Forbes article on 14 June 2011, source: http://www.forbes.com/sites/johnkotter/2011/06/14/think-youre-communicating-enough-think-again/

72 David Marquet in "Turn the Ship Around!" Penguin Group, 2012, pages 25 – 26.

73 "Getting Things Done: The Art of Stress-Free Productivity," Viking / Penguin Group, 2001, pages 18-19

74 David Marquet in "Turn the Ship Around!" Penguin Group, 2012, page 59

Chapter 4 Footnotes - Who is involved in transforming to Flow?

Chapter 5 Footnotes - The Flow Formula for Success

75 *Steve Jobs, see #37 on the following list: http://www.minterest.org/best-inspirational-quotes-by-steve-jobs/*

76 *Helen Keller, see: http://www.goodreads.com/quotes/12998-the-most-pathetic-person-in-the-world-is-some-one*

77 Tom DeMarco in his book "Slack: Getting Past Burnout, Busy Work, and the Myth of Total Efficiency" Random House, 2002, page 133

78 Donald Reinertsen as quoted in a blog post, see: http://blog.nwcadence.com/thoughts-on-principles-of-product-development-flow-part-1/

79 Proverbs 29:18, King James Version of the Bible

80 Proverbs 29:18, Darby Translation of the Bible

81 Paul DiModica in "Value Forward Selling" Johnson and Hunter, 2006, page 25

82 *Source: https://en.wikipedia.org/wiki/W._Edwards_Deming*

83 Jim Collins and William Lazier in "Beyond Entrepreneurship" Prentice Hall, 1992, pages 14-15

84 Jim Collins and William Lazier in "Beyond Entrepreneurship" Prentice Hall, 1992, page 15

85 See Wikipedia: https://en.wikipedia.org/wiki/Parkinson's_law

86 *Bryan Stolle in Forbes, source: http://www.forbes.com/sites/bryanstolle/2014/07/22/vision-without-execution-is-just-hallucination/*

87 See: http://www.agilemanifesto.org/principles.html

88 Aaron Shenhar and Dov Dvir in "Reinventing Project Management" Harvard Business School Press, 2006, page 208

Chapter 6 – Antipatterns that Block Flow

89 David Marquet in "Turn the Ship Around!" Penguin Group, 2012, page 11

90 David Marquet in "Turn the Ship Around!" Penguin Group, 2012, page 44

91 David Robertson in "Brick by Brick: How LEGO Rewrote the Rules of Innovation and Conquered the Global Toy Industry" Crown Publishing Group, a Division of Random House, 2013, pages 68 and 98

92 David Robertson in "Brick by Brick: How LEGO Rewrote the Rules of Innovation and Conquered the Global Toy Industry" Crown Publishing Group, a Division of Random House, 2013, page 285

93 David Robertson in "Brick by Brick: How LEGO Rewrote the Rules of Innovation and Conquered the Global Toy Industry" Crown Publishing Group, a Division of Random House, 2013, page 7

94 How Hardwired Is Human Behavior? By Nigel Nicholson in the July-August 1998 issue of HBR, see: https://hbr.org/1998/07/how-hardwired-is-human-behavior

95 David Robertson in "Brick by Brick: How LEGO Rewrote the Rules of Innovation and Conquered the Global Toy Industry" Crown Publishing Group, a Division of Random House, 2013, page 16

96 David Robertson in "Brick by Brick: How LEGO Rewrote the Rules of Innovation and Conquered the Global Toy Industry" Crown Publishing Group, a Division of Random House, 2013, page 116

97 Zig shared the story in a motivational tape series on selling over 30 years ago. Video of the "stinking thinking" story is on YouTube: https://www.youtube.com/watch?v=cRMogDrHnMQ

98 Stanford Business Professor Robert Sutton in his book "The No Asshole Rule: Building a Civilized Workplace and Surviving One That Isn't" Business Plus; Reprint edition (September 1, 2010)

99 Stanford Business Professor Robert Sutton in his book "The No Asshole Rule: Building a Civilized Workplace and Surviving One That Isn't" Business

Plus; Reprint edition (September 1, 2010); see: https://www.goodreads.com/work/quotes/2111894-the-no-asshole-rule-building-a-civilized-workplace-and-surviving-one-th

100 Stanford Business Professor Robert Sutton in his book "The No Asshole Rule: Building a Civilized Workplace and Surviving One That Isn't" Business Plus; Reprint edition (September 1, 2010); see: https://www.goodreads.com/work/quotes/2111894-the-no-asshole-rule-building-a-civilized-workplace-and-surviving-one-th

101 Jeff Sutherland, "The Power of Scrum" ScrumInc.com, 2011, page 112

102 Richard Sheridan in "Joy, Inc." Penguin Group, 2015, page 49

103 Timothy Rowe, founder of Cambridge Incubator

104 Daniel Pink in "Drive: the Surprising Truth about what Motivates Us" Penguin Group, 2009, page 142-143

105 Steven Kotler with Peter Diamandis in their book "Bold: How to Go Big, Create Wealth and Impact the World" Simon and Schuster, 2015, page 108

106 Steven Kotler with Peter Diamandis in their book "Bold: How to Go Big, Create Wealth and Impact the World" Simon and Schuster, 2015, see quote number 4273 at the following link: https://ffbsccn.wordpress.com/2012/07/04/some-of-my-highlighted-quotes-from-abundance-by-diamandis-and-kotler/

107 Steven Denning in "The Leader's Guide to Radical Management" Jossey-Bass, 2010, page 193

108 Steven Denning in "The Leader's Guide to Radical Management" Jossey-Bass, 2010, page 200

Chapter 7 - Disrupted Flow

109 Susan Cain in "Quiet: The Power of Introverts in a World that Can't Stop Talking" Random House, 2013, page 94

110 Gary Keller in "The One Thing" Bard Press, 2012, pages 34-35

111 Jeff Sutherland, "Scrum: A revolutionary approach to building teams, beating deadlines, and boosting productivity" Random House Business Books, 2014, see preview on Google Books at: http://tinyurl.com/m779ass

Chapter 8 - Training, Coaching and Mentoring

112 Simon Cinek in "Start with WHY" Penguin Group, 2009, page 99

113 Mihaly Csikszentmihalyi in "Good Business: Leadership, Flow, and the Making of Meaning" Penguin Group, 2003, page 116

Chapter 9 - Conclusion

114 Mihaly Csikszentmihalyi in "Good Business: Leadership, Flow, and the Making of Meaning" Penguin Group, 2003, page 107

115 Mihaly Csikszentmihalyi in "Good Business: Leadership, Flow, and the Making of Meaning" Penguin Group, 2003, page 113

116 Tom DeMarco in his book "Slack: Getting Past Burnout, Busy Work, and the Myth of Total Efficiency" Random House, 2002, page 134

117 Daniel Burrus in a speech to PMI-Western Michigan Chapter's Professional Development Day, March of 2014.

118 Daniel Burrus in his excellent book, "Flash Foresight" HarperCollins Publishers, 2011, pages 42-43

Appendix A – Flow Mini-case Studies

119
2. Mini-case: Steelcase InTandem SFA project
 Peter Diamandis in his book "Bold: How to Go Big, Create Wealth and Impact the World" Simon and Schuster, 2015, page 248
120
8. Mini-case: Successful use of the UVF and Flow with the PMI-Western Michigan Chapter (WMPMI, Project Management Institute)
 Peter Diamandis in his book "Bold: How to Go Big, Create Wealth and Impact the World" Simon and Schuster, 2015, page 99
121
10. Mini-case: Nature Publishing Group
 Jeff Sutherland in his book "Scrum: the Art of Doing Twice the Work in Half the Time" Crown Business, Random House, 2014, page 156

122 Kent Anderson, Jan 20 2015 blog post in the Scholarly Kitchen, see: https://scholarlykitchen.sspnet.org/2015/01/20/macmillan-springer-some-lessons-to-learn-some-twists-to-watch/

Appendix B Footnotes

123 See http://www.theglobeandmail.com/report-on-business/careers/management/a-companys-culture-has-to-come-from-within-or-it-will-fail/article14169921/?page=all

124 Arthur Shopenhauer, a 19th Century German Philosopher, see: https://www.brainyquote.com/quotes/quotes/a/arthurscho103608.html

125 Al Ries and Jack Trout, "The 22 Immutable Laws of Marketing" 1993, see: https://blog.kowalczyk.info/article/11e/Laws-of-marketing-20-hype.html

126 As witnessed by Andrew in a meeting, first hand.

127 *Andrew and Ted Kallman, aka the PMO Brothers.*

128 *Andrew and Ted Kallman, aka the PMO Brothers.*

129 Source: Shared in a presentation by Dr. Sutherland at SGLAS (Scrum Gathering Las Vegas) in 2013

130 Source: http://tinyurl.com/qgrbzr3

131 Yoh study (note: the link is broken and the report has been deleted by Yoh): http://www.yoh.com/AboutYoh/PressRoom/Press%20Releases/NewsItem?id=%7B9B8513C4-A6A6-4054-A8AD-9D59EA79FCDC%7D

132 Yoh study (note: the link is broken and the report has been deleted by Yoh): http://www.yoh.com/AboutYoh/PressRoom/Press%20Releases/NewsItem?id=%7B9B8513C4-A6A6-4054-A8AD-9D59EA79FCDC%7D

133 Source: Chinese Proverb

134 John Dehart, Founder of Nurse next Door, see his blog: http://www.johndehartblog.com/2010/02/25/culture-eats-process-for-breakfast/

135 Scrum Inc.'s Blog with Steve Denning, quote from Forbe's: http://www.forbes.com/sites/stevedenning/2012/04/17/the-case-against-agile-ten-perennial-management-objections/

136 John Dehart, Founder of Nurse next Door, see his blog: http://www.johndehartblog.com/2010/02/25/culture-eats-process-for-breakfast/

Morgan James
Speakers Group

www.TheMorganJamesSpeakersGroup.com

We connect Morgan James published authors with live and online events and audiences who will benefit from their expertise.

 Morgan James makes all of our titles available
through the Library for All Charity Organization.

www.LibraryForAll.org

9 781683 506454